What the Average Guy Is Thinking

Spread Love!!!

What the Average Guy Is Thinking

Relationship Rules
From a Regular Dude

Donald Thomas Jr.

Alpharetta, Georgia

ISBN: 978-0-9854980-0-9

Printed in the United States of America

♾ This paper meets the requirements of ANSI/NISO Z39.48-1992 (Permanence of Paper)

All scripture quotations are taken from the King James Version of the Holy Bible.

This book is dedicated to Mr. Donald Thomas Sr.

for teaching me to be a man.

To Mrs. Faber Thomas

for showing me what a real woman is.

To Donald O'Neal, Mckeithen, and Tarilynn Thomas

for being my motivation;

and to any woman who shared a relationship experience and a

life lesson with me that helped forge this book into existence.

TABLE OF CONTENTS

INTRODUCTION

Understanding relationships, especially in these days and times, is harder than solving a calculus problem, blindfolded, in a snowstorm, on a busy highway. Seriously, the gap between women and men can be bridged for some, but for most of us, understanding each other and finding that right mate sometimes seems impossible. Because of this, many of us seek guidance from outside sources: friends, family, church, television, internet, etc. Another popular source of guidance is books. Over the past few years, authors like Steve Harvey, Hill Harper, and several others have released books on relationships from a man's point of view. With their popularity, visibility, and big marketing budgets these books have done well and serve as gospel for many women. To their credit, these guys are awesome and offer something to the overall spectrum of figuring out our roles in relationships. However, even though I believe some things reign true for all men, a world famous comedian, actor, psychologist, singer, television journalist, or whatever is NOT who the average woman is dating.

The guys that YOU are dealing with on a day to day basis work at Wal-Mart, Fed-Ex, the ship yard, the construction site, the fire department, the accounting firm, or run their own landscaping company. Even though they are the same on some levels, the daily life of the men you encounter shapes him, molds him, and conditions him into someone quite different from the authors that have been giving you advice. Baby-Mama drama, pressures from work, and family obligations are very different when you're a millionaire as compared to when you're making five dollars above minimum wage. For that reason, I decided to write a book to give you the perspective of the "Average Joe." I seek to put our mindsets and issues on front street – not with the intention of belittling, causing controversy, gaining popularity, or bashing any particular gender — but with the sole purpose of bringing that man or woman that seems frustratingly miles away from you a little closer. So listen up, this is "What the Average Guy Is Thinking."

Chapter One

WHO ARE WE

In order to make anything perform to the best of its ability, you have to understand it. Many times in getting to know a person, we fail to actually *get to know a person*. Our forward progress is motivated by visual stimulation, verbal persuasion, emotional uproars, and actions that resemble acts of decency and kindness. For the most part, those things are needed and necessary, but those things can all be staged, faked, or orchestrated. Sometimes they can be a true representation of that person's inner makeup, but a lot of times it's the simple mechanics of the first few months of a relationship.

For example, an abusive man is not going to smack you in the face on the first date. If he did, you would be out the door in five seconds and back with the police in five minutes. It's when you have become attached to him after all those non-violent interactions and he has some kind of foundation established with you that he starts to grab on you and talk to you forcibly. Even though he bought you flowers the first week, took you on a two month anniversary picnic, and helped your mom with Thanksgiving dinner, doesn't change

1

the fact that he's crazy. The reason you didn't find out earlier about those issues is because you never tried to.

Many women in a relationship have the attitude of "if it ain't broke, don't fix it." You're all about the feelings. *After all the men that made you feel bad, you're just out searching to feel good again.* Instead, you should be looking for a man that's equally yoked to you. The first step in that process is to understand who you are, what your needs are, and what are your wants are. Pray about that, do some soul searching, and determine who you are. I could get into a sermon about that, but that's going to have to be in my next book. This book is from a man's perspective, so I'm going to need you all to figure out a way to figure out who you are. After you figure out who you are, you have to figure out who we are; and that I can help you with. Here's what you need to do…

John Doe Theory

When getting to know a man, you have to understand what being a man means. We are proud, masculine, egotistical beings. We are based on logic, and we aren't the best at handling our emotions. We are even worse at handling your emotions. If something stirs up a negative or uneasy emotion in us, either we punch it in the face, ignore it, or do something to stir up another emotion that counters it. *Things in our past tend to make us who we presently are to avoid facing those things again in the future.*

For example, if I dated someone that frequented the night clubs and she cheated on me in a relationship, every girl that resembles her is now a cheater and will get treated as such I will treat them without any respect or interest to avoid any possible attachment, or I will just avoid those type girls altogether. To be cliché, "One bad apple will spoil the whole bunch." In that situation, no matter how good of a woman you are, and no matter how well you treat me, the minute you put on your pumps to go out you become the enemy. It's not fair, and as we mature we handle it better, but I'm telling you that's how a lot of men think. To avoid you spinning your wheels on a man that will never let you get passed a certain point, I've developed a concept that I called the "John Doe Theory."

John Doe is a term used to describe a person or corpse that is unidentified. No one recognizes this person or knows who they are, and they have no form of instant identification. Whenever you meet someone, that person should be a John Doe to you. Even if they are a friend of yours, or a friend of a friend, if you have not been in a relationship with them before treat them as a John Doe.

Now, once a John Doe is found, the police begin an investigation to determine who this person is. They list his height, weight, race, eye and hair color, tattoos, scars, clothing, possessions, the location where he was found, and any other detail that may give a clue as to where to search for someone or something that will identify this man. As all the details are gathered, they're looked at closely and examined, and a search begins based off of the facts. What you have to realize is that the main factor in a John Doe case is that John Doe can't speak for himself, so who he is has to be determined by the naked truth. He can't open his mouth and say, "I'm a good father"; there have to be family pictures in his wallet of his children, a stamp on his hand from Chuck E. Cheese, or paid in full receipts from a daycare in his pocket. He can't just tell you how faithful of a husband he is and have you believe it, when his body was found in a motel under an assumed name. The thing about a John Doe is that who he says he is, good or bad, is irrelevant because he has to be objectively examined under hardcore facts. He can't persuade you or convince you, the truth will do all the talking.

The point is this: conversation rules the nation, and a lot of men have the gift of gab. Basically, they talk you right into where they want you to be. Remember, women are emotional, and soft words and compliments feel good to hear. The "I love you's" and "I'm thinking about you's" are readily accepted by a woman, and it feeds their desire to be loved. When that happens, they identify John Doe as their boyfriend, man, fiancé, or husband, but they haven't really gathered the facts needed to validate that. However, they don't require all the Facts, when they have allowed all the Feelings. You need to ask yourself the following questions: "What has this man shown me, that let me know he will be a good husband? What has taken place outside of a conversation that says he's looking to be married soon? Has there been enough opportunity for him to show up as a faithful boyfriend, or has this man simply put me in an emotional state that I'm enjoying too much to question?" Now don't get me wrong, I'm not saying to be overly pessimistic and nit-pick at every relationship, just make sure he's not handing you a fake I.D.

So how do you go about identifying your John Doe? You have to "tune in." When I get into my car and I turn on the radio, I have six selections for preset radio stations: number one is the hip-hop station number two R&B number three pop, and so on and so forth. These presets provide me with convenience. There are forty other stations in my area but these are the six that I prefer. I seldom go outside those stations unless I'm playing a CD. The station I prefer the most, that best suits me, is number one and they decrease in order. Now granted, 97.9 "The Box" in Houston is my favorite station in the world, but I can't receive its signal in

my area, so I have selected the best that I have access to.
Basically, if you go through my presets, it tells you a lot about
what kind of music I like and gives a pretty accurate account
of what style of music is my favorite by the station's format
and its position on my ordering. Now on occasion I visit
Atlanta, and when I hop into my rental car and turn on the
radio, I have to locate a whole new set of presets. I like jazz,
but its not available back home, so ill put a jazz station in the
rotation and enjoy it while I can. Now how does that relate to
understanding your potential man? Here's how.

Listen Live

   As men, we have "presets" or predispositions. Those
predispositions determine our preferences and "what we
listen to." In other words: who we are interested in, who we
date, and how we act in a relationship. My predispositions are
based of my environment, so as much as I would like a
female doctor as a wife (i.e. jazz station), there just aren't any
available in my area (i.e. ghettos, middle class neighborhoods,
small towns). Women are our music. If hip-hop is number
one and Country is number six, I can very well enjoy you if
you're "Country" but I may not be as into you as I would my
"hip-hop." Knowing that will help you determine how fast
you should move forward in a relationship with me.

   Every guy has an idea of what his 97.9 "The Box" girl is
like, but we will settle for the best station that we can catch
(but be weary of not being his 97.9 girl). The trap a lot of
women fall into is that they try to change our station. They
want us to consider another genre of music, but if I'm a
heavy metal listener, you're going to have a hard time getting
me to buy into your gospel station. The plan can't be to
change our station; instead you need to perform "station

identification." Once you've learned our stations, ask yourself if you are you on our dial. If not, be wise and move on. Another fact about presets is that it's hard to upgrade our station listing without changing our environment. I can never fully appreciate jazz until I up and move to Atlanta. Getting bits and pieces of that station through a scratchy signal won't ever truly please me. If my environment and surroundings are still hectic and not where I want to be as a man, I can't appreciate you over all my background noise. In that situation, allow me time to get myself together and get closer to your signal. Going forward, take time to talk to us and learn our history. Find out where we come from, where we are, and where we're going. If we are at a hip-hop stage in our lives, let us mature into gospel music if that's what you prefer. Because at the end of the day, we still have the option to turn the radio off.

Chapter Two

HOW WE SEE YOU

Eye of the Beholder

Extreme Prejudice

During the civil rights movement, those who ignorantly promoted segregation and racism kept their beliefs simple: if you weren't white, you were lesser. It didn't matter how many degrees you had, how much money you made, or how many times you forgave and tried to show love, all they saw was darker skin and instantly hated that particular individual. To be black, was a label; an identifying mark that placed you into a predetermined category. Even years after segregation was over, those who believed in it, refused to adjust to it. They were programmed and set in their ways. What one must understand is that, this programming process did not take place over night. It takes generations to instill such beliefs, behaviors, and attitudes. The same is true for the beliefs of males when it comes to how we view women.

It takes generations of older brothers, cousins, uncles, grandpas, and most of all fathers–both absent and present–to create the mindset of the men you have to deal with on a day to day basis. His way of thinking comes from what he has seen or was taught–whether his thinking is barbaric, and he wants to drag you around by your hair, or his thinking is progressive, and he supports your career-driven life.

Thankfully, there are many cases where a person is raised in a negative thinking environment, and goes against the grain. Cases where a male is exposed to generations of ignorance, only fuels him to be the exact opposite of that. A person's individuality, combined with his relationship with God, can propel him to break those generational curses. He can then start a fresh new generation of men in his family, beginning with him and passed down to his seeds. But whether his way of thinking is like Barack Obama or Captain Caveman, your progression with him is still based on how he perceives you. When you cross our path or engage in those first few conversations, we form an opinion of you. We get an impression of who you are and who you could be to us. Let's discuss some popular classifications when men get that "*first impression*" of a woman.

Housewife – This is the most classic stereotype of women. The traditional stay-at-home, cook, clean, and raise the children type of woman. Yeah, I know it doesn't sound appealing when you say it that way, especially in 2012, but for many men it's a label that we place on certain females we encounter. It's the thinking that this particular woman is probably not going to be working a job making the "big bucks." She's probably not going to have an issue taking up all the household chores. She may carry eighty-five to ninety percent of the responsibility of seeing to the welfare of the children. I know it's somewhat of an unfair label but surprisingly, many women like this tag placed on them and welcome that role with open arms. It's very traditional, and it's a very well defined classification established in many marriages. Often men base these classifications on a woman's employment, education, goals (planned or lacking), economic status, and personality traits. As with anything though, it goes back to the individual's upbringing.

I grew up in the South, and my family hails from small, religious, old fashioned, country towns. It is very common in these areas to have a husband that drives 18-wheelers, works offshore, or is employed by a job that is very time-consuming or physically demanding. Because of this, his role in the family is limited to breadwinner, and the responsibility of maintaining the household is left to the woman. This role is very demanding, and requires a lot of strength on her part. The issue over the years is that the perception of this role leads society to believe that the woman who plays this part is lesser. If a person's motivation is money, they're going to think that working a lesser paying job, or not working at all, makes the housewife less of a contributor to the relationship. In actuality, your role is just as significant as or even more significant than that of your breadwinning partner. Once you've identified that you are viewed as a potential housewife, find out what your potential man thinks a housewife is. Are you his Wilma Flintstone, Florida Evans, or his Peggy Bundy?

Knowing whether or not you have been tagged with this label can be identified in several ways. Does he trust you with non-domestic matters? Does he respect your opinion or even seek your opinion on major issues? Does he assume you're going to go along with decisions that he makes? Does he take your plans for your life into consideration when he's discussing all of his future goals? Does he think he knows what you want all the time and what should make you happy?

These questions can point out the kind of guy you don't want to be "Mrs. Housewife" for. All in all, the role of housewife a.k.a. "Life Management Specialist and Ambassador to Family Domestication," is the backbone of America. You're raising our children, and a lot of times raising us. Don't avoid this title; just make sure your mate understands what this title really means to both of you.

Trophy Wife – This is "Ms. Pretty," "Ms. High Maintenance," "Ms. All That." She is the stereotypical high school cheerleading captain, homecoming queen, "most likely to be Miss America" girl. This is the female that every guy agrees: "I'd make her my wife if she let me," strictly because of how attractive she is. First, you have to understand something: women are the most beautiful creations God has ever made. When a man is exposed to, what we consider to be, the very best of that creation we get a little bit beside ourselves. It can go from an infatuation to a downright obsession. It becomes less about how good of a relationship it is and more about the pride we take in how it looks. As men, we have a confidence meter and we subconsciously rate how attractive a woman we are able to obtain. Eventually you'll learn that any good man can acquire any good woman, but most of us learn that much later in life. Mostly, we tend to look for the best that we can acquire inside our league, if you will.

The trophy wife symbolizes a woman that is either at the very top of our league or completely exceeds our own expectations. She's our esteem booster, our prized acquisition, and our statement that says "Hey, look what I did!" Guys tend to basically worship this woman, and will go through great lengths to keep her. What's the downside? This relationship tends to be superficial. It lacks any real substance, it's very external, and it doesn't carry a lot of internal, emotional make up. The man who has a trophy will go to great lengths to keep her, and will go to even greater lengths to not let her leave. Think about that for a second. As flattering as you may think it is to be worshipped, I suggest you think again. Anything that is worshipped besides God is a disaster waiting to happen. The truth is that all God's people are beautiful and should be respected, nurtured, and catered to equally. Although we are attracted to each other on different levels, the intensity of love should be based on actions, connection, affection, sacrifice, etc.; not complexion and cup size. A man who is that intensely taken by your physical features, and values you on only those details has some issues of his own. Either they don't really care about you, or they have low self-esteem and find justification through you. Occasionally this is one of the personalities that leads to stalker behavior. My advice to you is if you find yourself in this type of relationship, take pride in knowing you're the bomb, and then immediately get yourself out of that relationship. I would suggest you break it off in a public place.

Homegirl – We all want our mate to be our best friend, but how many of us want our best friend to be our mate? I mean think about it, we all have that friend that we can go have a platonic outing with. This person is that friend that you honestly never looked at "that way." Some people cater to your personality in a way that makes you extremely comfortable around them. They are the people that are fun, dependable, trustworthy, humorous, and always pleasant to be around. These are the people that are easy to talk to. You often find yourself seeking their advice, using their ears as receivers for your problems and their shoulders as deposit tanks for your tears. These relationships provide a certain level of comfort that's often not reproduced easily. Because these people have been there in the ups and downs, a frequent misconception is that this friendship can transform into a relationship. Sometimes it can. However, a lot of times the attraction to this type of friend is the subconscious wish that the person you want to be in a relationship with treated you the way the friend does. We get caught up in the personality of that person and not the actual person. Usually it's a knee jerk reaction, or a rebounding based situation that allows these friends to venture off into unchartered territory. *It's only natural that when you get let down by people a lot, that you would develop an interest in someone who has never let you down.*

The truth of the matter is this: if I never looked at you that way before, I'm probably not going to start now. Even if we somehow have a mental lapse and manage to cross some previous boundary, I'm going to snap back to my senses rather quickly. You have to remember, women are the emotional ones. I'm probably not going to build this bond with you over the years that can transition me from your buddy to your hubby. If I didn't look at you that way when I met you in sixth grade math class, I'm probably not going to change now. Maybe in high school, when I struggled with puberty, I might have said some things to you that was outside of "homie" status, but that was a rough time for all of us. If you and a guy are cool, I mean really cool, it's a contradiction to think he has the hots for you. So you see ladies, we have a friend zone too.

Hoochie – I have learned in life that a person's perception is their reality. It doesn't matter if it's true or not; if I believe it to be, then so it is. For that reason, your reputation and image does speak for you, so be very careful of how you carry yourself. Granted, no one can or should judge anyone, so if you want to wear what you want to wear, or hangout wherever you like that's your business. All I'm saying is if I see a man in a navy blue uniform, holstering a gun, with a badge pinned on him, sitting inside a car with red and blue lights on the roof, I'm probably not going to run a stop sign in front of him. Even though I've never met him in person or held a conversation with him, I'm going to err on the side of caution and react to him based on the details I see. So, feel free to wear you're an all-black cat suit with thigh high boots, but you're not going to be meeting my mother anytime soon.

I've heard women say that just because they wear short skirts or low cut shirts, that "don't make them a whore," and that's true. I'm just saying that if you have the right to wear what you want, I have the right to think what I want. I'm just playing it safe. If I go to your house and you have a Pit Bull in the yard with a spiked collar, I'm not going to be as quick to enter as I would if you had a miniature poodle with a pink bow on its head. The reality is that certain details are a result of certain traits. It's no different than if I approached you and I had gold teeth with neck tattoos. Are you going to believe me when I tell you I'm in my last semester of law school? No! The first thing in your mind is "look at that thug, rapper, or d-boy," which is probably a fair assessment.

There was a line in a movie that said, "You can't turn a hoe into a housewife." I've never seen that quote in any of Gandhi's teachings, never heard it uttered in a sermon by Dr. Martin Luther King Jr., and I'm pretty sure it's not in the Bible, but men still tend to believe it. We might try to associate with you knowing you have a promiscuous reputation, but it's not in the interest of planning a future with you. No man wants a loose woman. Not one of us. Even though you may not be, as long as we think you are, we are going to treat you as such.

I do have to admit that we do need women to be appealing to a certain degree to get us to notice them, and I'm not saying there's anything wrong with dressing sexy, but it's about tastefulness. The other concern is how you carry yourself. Every guy likes to be flirtatious with a woman and it's a very good feeling to receive attention from the opposite sex, but what will diminish that feeling is non-exclusivity. Your compliments and smiling gestures don't carry as much weight when every other guy in the office gets the same treatment. Our thinking is: "Why should I make her my woman when everybody else gets the same attention?" It's not always about us thinking your promiscuous, it's mostly about us believing that you have an insecurity that requires you to search for attention. *Women are a rare breed to us. They shine in moments of weakness, where they allow us to take care of them, but they also shine in moments of strength where they are confident and complete, and require us to work for and earn their attention.* Clothes, promiscuity, attitudes, flirting, and swagger will guarantee you attention, but it probably won't guarantee you a healthy relationship.

Now Hiring...

When guys are in a relationship we tend to pick a lane that's familiar to us. We look for that situation that fits into what we currently have going on or what lines up with what were comfortable with. If we have kids, those women that have good parenting and homemaking skills will appeal to us. If we are up and coming musicians, then a woman with industry connections seems like the jackpot mate we've been looking for. As a result, you could find yourself in a relationship not because of who you are (good and faithful woman), but because of what you are (housekeeper, accountant, etc.). The downside to this is that in most cases your job is your purpose in the man's life. Therefore, when your job is complete and there is no longer a need for your services, you no longer have a purpose and are often times terminated. Take a look at some popular job titles that we sometimes give women that keep them gainfully employed in relationships. Take a closer look at the job description, then compare it to your current and former relationships and see if you've been working on a relationship, or just working.

Nanny – There has been a lot of slack over the past years about men being deadbeat dads, but don't get it twisted; we love our kids. A lot of men fall short in their responsibility because of pressure, immaturity, insecurity, or just plain ignorance, but it's seldom because we don't love our kids. With that being said, nothing makes a woman more attractive to us than a woman that steps in and handles her business when it comes to our kids. If you're the "help Susie with her homework, take Brandon to football practice, and change Sally's diaper" type of girl, welcome to our world. Of course, you can't be with a man and not be involved with his kids if he has them. That would be wrong but beware of being the fill-in for their mom when it's his day to have them. A surefire sign that you've become the nanny is when you're doing all these tasks and he's nowhere around. Family time should include the whole family. If the father is working, or has previous obligations that make him unavailable when he has kids, then he should wait to get them when he is available. Otherwise you'll end up playing nanny all the time.

The variation on this job title exists with those guys who are single parents and have their children full time. Single parent dads contract women for a longer period of time, but it is still a temporary form of employment. It may take seventeen years for the contract to end, but it still bears the threat of ending. Being a single parent is hard for a woman. It is borderline impossible for a man, but many of us do it. I have done the single parent thing a few times since my divorce, and I know for a fact that the women I dated when I didn't have my kids were the women that were best for me. When I had my kids, I dated the women that were best for them. A single dad raising three kids on his own is very, very, very attractive to a woman; especially women who have not-so-great baby fathers of their own. It's very easy to get caught up in having a family and not realize that having a family doesn't mean you have a relationship. Let that marinate. As long as my kid's needs were met, I was cool, but in time I failed to maintain the woman's needs because the woman was never my priority. As expected, we didn't break up, they quit.

Treasurer – Beware of people when money is their motivation. The Bible clearly states, "For the love of money is a root of all kinds of evil" (I Timothy 6:10). When greed, pride, vanity, and selfishness fill your heart, you do what it takes to keep your pockets fat. What greater gift is there than a "money tree?" If you're financing his recording sessions, covering him on his child support payments, or simply going half with him on the light bill, of course he's going to have time for you. However, when he gets that record deal with Bad Boy, do you believe he's going to tell Diddy he needs two plane tickets to New York, or will you be following him on Twitter to see where he is? There's nothing wrong with teaming up with someone you care about to make ends meet, especially in today's economy, but when he's able to afford his own place, it all of a sudden becomes clear why he never wanted to sign on your current lease.

Another point is that many women take great pride in their independence. They congratulate themselves on their degrees, promotions, accomplishments, and delight in being able to say they're established. If you've got it, flaunt it, but remember that money can't buy love. Guys don't really get the concept of not accepting a gift. If you bought most guys a pair of Jordan's, Madden 2014, and season passes for his favorite football team, you're going to shoot straight to the top of his list. In fact, you're going to stay on the top of that list well after his team gets put out of the playoffs, but don't overlook the fact that he still has a list. The truth is that after all that spending, his team could go on to win a Super Bowl ring, but you still won't even have a promise ring. When I say know your value, I don't mean in dollars.

A clue to finding out if you're working this job is to think about all the good times you've had together and determine how many of those times were related to, or in anticipation of, some sort of financial benefit. How often is money poured into this relationship? What other role do you play in this relationship? Do you have another role, or can this relationship constitute as a reference on your resume for the job you applied for at the bank?

Sex Therapists – If money is the greatest motivator of sin, then lust is definitely a close second. Sex is a major factor in relationships, and if someone tells you it's not they're lying their butt off! If they're not lying – never mind, they're lying. I don't know if you guys knew this, but let me share a little secret with you: men love sex! Our first attraction to you is a physical one. We look at your face and your body (not necessarily in that order) and get attracted to you well before we ever know your name. Sometimes, your physical features become part of the internal nickname we give you (i.e. big-booty Sheila, heavy-set Tracy). As single guys, and sometimes not single, we like to keep "old faithful" around to cover our lapses in sexual encounters. These are the girls who don't tell us no when it comes to sex; the women who love or lust us so badly, they feel justified when we sleep together. Every guy at some point has that girl that they can call at two thirty in the morning and she'll answer the phone. In her mind, he's calling because he misses her and wants some quality time. She believes this is an act of faithfulness because you could have been anywhere in the world, but instead you're there with her. The reality is that we were trying to be elsewhere and that didn't quite work out; something old is better than nothing new.

I know this sounds raw, and men don't really think that way about women (*Wink-wink*). Just to be on the safe side, ask yourself these questions: When you and your man met, how long was it before you were sexually active; honestly? Did he become more or less aggressive in his pursuit of you after you started having sex? Is he more eager to do things when he knows it's going to result in sex? Does he "expect" sex from you or is it just an added benefit that you control and he just lucks out whenever you decide he's earned it? What would his reaction be if you told him you no longer wanted to have sex until after you were married? Without trying to judge anyone, I'm simply saying that *sex tends to be a natural occurrence between couples that love each other, but love is not a natural occurrence between couples that sex each other.* I consider myself to be a pretty decent guy and I have had these sex-based relationships several times throughout my life, and I know that my intentions for those females was never to marry them. Sex got my attention, but not my respect. I'm not saying you can't turn a whore into a housewife, but it's hard as hell to turn an emotionally starved, promiscuous, low self-esteem, sexually justified individual into an equally yoked partner. Please check your job description!

Chapter Three

IT'S A FAMILY AFFAIR

A lot of times, women get an inaccurate reading of a guy because she bases her opinion on how he interacts with his kids and his own family. If he's a "momma's boy," they either think he will cater to them as a woman as he does his mom, or maybe that she has to baby him to acquire him. Sometimes, a guy is so involved in his kids life you just can't imagine him not being an excellent father to your child. Nothing makes a woman's eye twinkle more watching a passionate father at work, thinking that that's the image of the man she wants in her household. For the most part, a lot of men are truthfully represented in the way they interact with their family. The catch is that you're not family–yet. And if I'm allowed to quote another cliché: "blood is thicker than water." Sometimes the roles you admire can become an obstacle. Sometimes the very thing that drew you in will keep you out. Don't get me wrong, I'm not trying to turn everything into a negative, I'm just trying to inform you for your own protection. Let's examine the good and bad, the up's and downs, and the various roles that guys and girls play in a family.

Mother Dearest – If there is ever a strong bond between a man and a woman, it's that of a mother and son. Even if there seems to be a disconnection in certain cases, don't get confused; a man will still go off on you if you talk about his momma. Often, a negative relationship between a man and his mother is just an emotional outburst of the man either blaming the person he's closest to for some sort of failure in his life, or him just not receiving all the "nurturing" he thinks he deserves from this never ending fountain of affection and validation. I mean think about it, men are not the most emotional creatures walking the earth, but they spend their first nine months of life attached to (what is for some) the only true emotional connection they will ever encounter. It's only natural that they have a longing for the purest love they have ever known. Where do you fit in all of this?

The first thing to be aware of is that mom can make or break you. If the mother-in-law to be adores you, and thinks you are the best thing for her son since his kindergarten teacher, she will campaign for you. You will be invited to all the family functions directly. You will get all the up-to-date reports of the son's current dates with other women and phone calls from new females. You will be the topic of discussion for every visit the son makes to "dear old mom." From the outside looking in, you're going to think that you're a shoe-in for the role of daughter-in-law. However, this book is about what we as men are thinking, not you or our mommas, so pay attention.

News Flash! We don't like our moms in our personal life, and for several reasons. We have habits and history that is not for our mothers to know about. I'm totally uncomfortable with my mom having the thought that I'm a freaky, kinky, and risqué type of guy, no matter how true it is. Also, if we haven't given you a title, don't accept the one she gives you, because unless you're dating our mom, her status upgrade for you is worthless. The biggest factor is that we don't want the inconvenience of having to deal with a relationship between you and our mothers after the relationship between us is over. That's just another form of commitment that we are not trying to endure.

I can remember one girl telling me, "You can't control who your mom talks to, just because you and I don't talk anymore doesn't mean I have to end my relationship with her. I can still see her if I want to." I guess in a civilized society such as ours, that's true, but when I made the phone call to my mother and told her how hurt I was by the ending of that relationship, and how upset I was with her for exposing me to continued hurts, she lost that girl's number quicker than five dollars at the blackjack table. Why? Because at the end of the day, no matter how much she loves you, she loves me more. Remember that the reason she loves you so much to begin with is because you represented something positive for her beloved son. Once you become a negative to her son, you become a negative to her as well, no matter how nice she is to you on the phone.

The second thing to be aware of is that even though many moms raise their sons to be better men while in relationships, other mothers raise spoiled rotten, co-dependent brats that walk around acting like grown men. These are the men that can't clean, cook, shop, budget, or even think for themselves. I think the term most popular is "Baby Boys" or "Momma's Boys." These men are easy to obtain because all you have to do are the things they don't do, which is everything. They have been raised to have a woman (mom) do everything for them and they can barely function without someone in that role. These are the guys that open their doors to you, but unfortunately it's so you can clean their house and not for any real benefit to you. These guys will treat you well and show you the affection you desire, and they are sincerely grateful for all that you bring to the table, especially dinner. The downside to this relationship is that when the duties and chores are gone, so is the interest and enthusiasm. Be careful in the process of housekeeping, not to become the housekeeper, and not having any other role in the relationship other than the girl who covers for mom on her day off. If you're going to do for your man, that's fine, just don't do what he's not willing or capable to do for himself. You should be able to establish a foundation based on your character, not your cooking.

Baby Mama Drama – I was previously married, and had three beautiful kids as a result of that marriage. Since my divorce, my kids have lived with me for extended amounts of time. I've done, and am currently doing, the single parent thing. I know going into a relationship that I have "baggage," which is a term I hate, but you know what I mean. Unfortunately, when I got ready to move into a relationship and I reached down to pick up my bags there were four instead of three: one bag for each of my kids and one for their mother. That's right, my baggage not only consisted of my kids for another woman to deal with, but it also enlisted the presence of the baby mama. I do understand that the baby mama's involvement in my life is to be controlled and regulated by me, but you need to understand how to handle yourself to not allow the ex to pull the strings that will put you in the same position as her–an ex. You have to remember that misery loves company and even though she may no longer want me, that doesn't mean she's a fan of you having me. Dealing with a baby mama can be peaceful sometimes; there are, of course, times when it's downright nerve-racking, but when the next girl and the ex-girl are both involved, it's almost always awkward.

There are a few keys to creating a happy environment when you're in a relationship with a guy that has kids (and subsequently, a mother of those kids). First off, you have to be honest with yourself as to whether you can and are willing to deal with this situation. Some women just don't want a guy with baggage. If that's you, then by all means express that and let both of us move on. Secondly, you need to communicate what you don't like or have an issue with and why. I'll be the first to admit, guys are stupid sometimes and we honestly don't know something's wrong until you tell us. My problem used to be that I allowed my ex-wife to have too much control over me after our divorce. She would use the kids as leverage because she knew I wouldn't let them be stuck in the middle of any drama. However, it put a strain on the current girl because she had to always adjust to me jumping through hoops to appease the kid's mother. As far as I knew, I thought the current woman was handling everything just fine, but she wasn't and she never told me. She figured I should've just known what my ex was doing to us. Uh, no.

Women are very smart, and when they're being deceitful or working a plan, most guys are defenseless. Ladies, when the baby mama implements her plan, we need you to be on the counter-offensive and protect us. Also, avoid letting her external drama become *our* internal drama. The most important factor is the welfare of the children. If you're building a good relationship with my kids and fulfilling their mother's role in her absence, then I'll make absolutely sure you're properly respected. Now granted, you should be respected anyway, but I'm just saying that when you pick up another woman's slack, she shouldn't treat you as anything less than a partner in the raising of her children. What you don't want to do is be standoffish with the kids. That's a sign of selfishness and immaturity. Just play your role and let time be the test for both you and me. If you're playing your role, you then have the right to say, "This is what I don't like and this is what I need you to do."

As men, we know that what you do to help us is under your own free will and out of love, and we do respect it and appreciate it. Therefore, once you give us a step by step man-proof list of instructions to follow, you will have both informed and educated us on how to handle the situation. In the end, we should be able to survive due to the established level of comfort and respect. There's no better source to tell us how to handle a woman than another woman.

Baby Daddy Drama – If you think dealing with our baby mamas is bad, you are leaps and bounds away from the headache of dealing with your baby daddy. Dealing with a woman in these situations seems worse, but it's really not. In most cases, a woman's drama stems from an emotional place, which can be sympathized and empathized with, but a guy's drama is usually straight pride, ignorance, ego, and even barbarism. Now, there are a lot of cases, where the guy is a victim, or he's trying to protect his children. Those are the exceptions, but I'm not dealing with that issue, I'm addressing that 6'0", 250lb, walking container of foolishness you call an ex. I've dealt with baby daddies, and I've been the baby daddy someone else had to deal with; not pretty on either side. However, it served as an informative and educational proving ground for one of the most interesting chapters you're ever going to read in your life. The key to Baby Daddy drama is information, identification, resignation, and realization.

Information: Relationships today have changed. As a society, when we meet a person of interest, our initial conversations have evolved into something very unique. Way back in the day, you asked a girl who her parents were to seek permission to court her. Then a few decades later, you asked a lady what's her name and her sign. In the 80s, you sought a home phone number, which became a beeper number, which became a cell phone number. Nowadays, we ask if you are on Facebook or Twitter. Those are some rather drastic changes, but it's not the only dynamic that has been altered by the hands of time.

These days it seems like everyone has a child or children, and dating is not just about you, but about your preset family. With "single with kids" being such a common status, the condition of that situation should not be foreign to the conversation of anyone you are seriously considering dating or committing to. In reference to dealing with a baby daddy, please offer us honest information as to who you are forever linked to through a child. Please understand that this is not a request to get in your business; but simply an enquiry as to exactly what we are dealing with. I think everyone is an individual and should be able to live their life free from another person's involvement, but when you share in the creation of life, you are forever involved. So as the new guy, I would appreciate if you just laid down a few basic details that would paint an accurate picture of what your situation is. What type of information? I'm glad you asked that question.

If you and your baby daddy are cool, have a civil agreement about each of your responsibilities in reference to your child, and are both respectable adults, then you can just say that you have a kid with a guy you're no longer with, but you guys get along. And in that case, that's honest and sufficient. However, if your baby daddy is currently stalking you, under a restraining order, and has held you and the children hostage within the past six months, maybe you shouldn't tell me, "My baby daddy be tripping sometimes, but we alright." That's not exactly the whole truth. I understand that your business is your business, but when this brother shows up with an ice pick and duct tape, your business instantly becomes my business. For the record, recognized relationship statuses are single, engaged, married, divorced, or legally separated. The following relationship statuses are not acceptable: it's complicated, kinda-sorta, on and off, just roommates, hanging around for the kids, or he's with me, but I ain't with him.

When you have a kid with someone, the introduction of an outsider can be complicated, so both parties need to come to an agreement and settle into that agreement before you bring someone into that situation. Don't selfishly involve me in your life and mask what you have going on. If you tell me what your situation is and I choose to continue on with you, then that's on me. At least you've allowed me the chance to choose under my own free will knowing all the info. In a nutshell, information is simply knowledge of your situation, and knowledge is power. Factors like the father not being allowed to visit his kids can't just be thrown out there lackadaisically because it leaves us with questions. Is the father not allowed to see his kids because he doesn't support them financially, or is it because he has a new girlfriend and you're bitter? Those details give me insight as to whether or not I want to deal with you at all. If you think I'm being distant, it's because I have questions that I'm waiting to get answered. It's the same questions you should want answered when you find out I had a kid I haven't seen in three years. Can you say red flag (For the record, that's just hypothetical; I don't have any long lost kids. Don't be trying to get me on Maury Povich)?

<u>Identification:</u> This is very important. Once you have shared all the relevant information, we can identify the

former man in your life for who he is. I can then identify what your needs are in that area and if I'm capable of meeting those needs. What do I mean? Check it out: if he doesn't work, doesn't help you take care of your kid, and is seriously not trying to change that situation, then I know I have the opportunity to step in and become that male replacement in your life and your child's. In this case, we will have identified him as a "Deadbeat Dad." However, if your kid's father is really supportive, respectful of you, and a mature, responsible adult, then he'll garner the tag of the "Kid's Father" (and not the dreadful term "baby daddy").

If your partner in procreation is the one that is more concerned with your current relationships rather than the relationship he has with his kids, he's going to be labeled as the "Bitter-Baby-Daddy"(a male version of a woman scorned). I call those guys "Menvious;" a man who's envious of your current relationship. Menvious males always want to argue with you and point out flaws in you and the current man, and they are usually the biggest supporters of drama. There are also those guys who try to manipulate you through the kids. These guys use their words, strategic actions, and overly accommodating requests to keep you where they want you: single. These guys disguise their motives and mask their intentions. To you it looks like they are trying to be a good father, but to us they are just trying to be a nuisance. For example, the guy who wants his kids all the time, but requires you to drop them off and pick them up and he lives three hours away. Or, the guy who will have his children all week, but just can't seem to keep them on Friday and Saturday nights, or what would be potential date nights for you. This guy is what I like to call the "Magician," because he gives off the illusion of being a good guy but really is trying to make your new relationships disappear.

And last but not least, some of us are unlucky enough to date the girl who has kids for the guy I call the "Soul mate." This brother is the brother that has emotionally touched a woman in a way that no other man has even come close to. This is not the guy you loved, this is the guy you were *in love* with, and still are to some degree. This guy can do no wrong, and even if he did wrong, it wouldn't matter because he holds a very special place in your heart. This is the guy whose pictures you can't seem to throw away; the one who stands next to you in your imaginary family portrait. When I was young, I used to be threatened by the guy that took your virginity, but as I grew older I became concerned of the guy that took your heart, i.e. the soul mate. The problem with the soul mate is obvious: he can tell you what to do because deep down inside you still desire to make him happy. He keeps you from being complete in a new relationship because a big portion of you is still with him. I've seen this brother up close and personal, and its damn near amazing to watch him work.

One of my closest female friends battled with this type of guy for years. All my good, concerned, honest, and supportive advice did nothing but provoke a few "I feel ya's" and head nods, and then it was right back to the same routine. Remember, women are emotional not rational, so it didn't matter what made sense; it mattered what made her feel like she was living the life she longed for, even if it was a lie. And to the fellas that are reading this book, please don't underestimate this brother. It doesn't matter what he looks like, dresses like, smells like, or thinks like. It doesn't matter if he's unemployed, in jail, on crack, married, or even dabbling in the occult; if he has her heart, it's a wrap.

Okay, so now we know who we're dealing with, let's discuss how we're going to deal with them.

<u>Realization:</u> This is simple. In this step, I need to sit down with you and have an open, honest, consequence-free conversation where we lay down all the facts of our relationship and outlying situation, and we both agree that "this" is what we're dealing with. We both need to have clarity as to who and what your baby daddy is to you and come to the conclusion that it is what it is. At that point, if we decide we can continue, and it's worth dealing with, then we implement the next step: Resignation.

<u>Resignation:</u> When you resign from a job, four things happen. First, you decide you no longer want to work there. Second, you secure a new job. Thirdly, you notify your current job that you're leaving. Lastly, you quit. Well, when you resign from your baby daddy, it's the same thing. Let's look at what I mean.

Remember, the first step is to decide you no longer want to work there. This is not just about you being in a relationship with your ex, it's also about being in a certain situation with your ex. If you are in a relationship and it's just not working, it's simply a matter of saying you want to move on, but what if you are dealing with the "deadbeat dad" or the "magician?" In the case of the deadbeat, women tend to become mother and father. Ladies end up having to work to pay the bills, cook dinner, and still get lil'man to the barbershop before six o'clock. It's a very hard situation, but you guys make up your mind it's not going to break you and you handle it. When you're dealing with the magician, you desire your kids to have a good relationship with their father, so you take the steps to insure that happens. Even though it can be an obvious inconvenience, a woman will sacrifice her own happiness and desires for her children.

The problem the new man in your life faces is getting you to fully resign and stop "moonlighting." When I step into your life and you know I'm serious and I'm there for the long haul, you have to decide that you are ready to work with me; that the old job is no longer for you. It's very hard to work two jobs. I'm not saying you cut off contact with your former employer. No, you don't have to burn those bridges at all. What I'm saying is that you can no longer fulfill that job description.

If you have become mother and father as a result of a deadbeat, you have to let go and let someone help you. As a man, if I decide to be in your life, I have to be in your kid's life too, and most men desire to be that father figure. The issue is that you have developed a mindset where you can't count on a man and it's on you to get it done. That mindset is hard for a woman to let go of once it's instilled. You have to consciously let go of all that responsibility and share it with us.

Women have a comfort zone in which they will give leeway to a pee-wee football coach, the guy that cuts hair in the neighborhood, or the counselor at the YMCA. A man can take your kid to the barbershop, teach him how to catch a football, or show him how to put on a tie. You allow that and love every moment of it. For some reason though, when the invite comes for "Dads & Daughters Day" at school, or the "Father & Sons" weekend camping trip with the boy scouts, you pause. Those events that signify the role of father subconsciously scare you into thinking that I will evade the job like the previously discussed individual, and you then go into survival mode. If I'm going to ever be that, you have to let me be that. I understand you have been mom and dad, but you have to understand that you don't always have to be. When it comes to the magician in your life, you have to feel okay with establishing a system. You have to get comfortable with the newfound help in your life that allows you to have a life. If the new man helps with the kids during the week, or adds additional income that allows you to afford a babysitter on the weekend, then challenge that baby daddy to step up and be more conveniently available for his kids. These changes can only take place once you fully decide you are ready to resign.

In the case of the "soul mate" and the "bitter baby daddy," it's an emotional detoxification. In one instance you have to decide to no longer be angry and the other you have to decide to no longer be happy. You have to make up your mind that the negative individual in your life is no longer going to have power over you, and can no longer make you upset. Even if you have to resort to a restraining order in those extreme cases, you have to do what you have to do and trust us to support and protect you. In the case of the guy that you're crazy about, you simply have to be ready to let go. You cannot harp on the past if you intend for me to be your future.

Now, the next step is to secure a new job. This simply means you have to redefine your role and properly define mine. You have to learn how to only be a mom. You have to learn how to allow yourself to have a life. You have to learn how to not put up with it anymore. You have to learn how to be his ex. You are in the process of changing employment, look at your I.D. badge closely and see what it says. It no longer reads single parent, taken advantage of, punching bag, side chick, or manipulated. As a matter of fact, you now have one of those stick on badges that say, "Hello, my name is:_____" Now you have the power to feel in the blank. Once you know your role, it will help me better understand mine.

The next step is to notify the former employee. You have to issue a two week notice. If you have to adjust your kids schedule with the magician, it can be a two month notice. In the case of the deadbeat, it can be a two minute notice. In matters of the heart like with the soul mate, that may end up being a two year notice, but I'm praying for you. The benefit of this step is that you are making an announced statement that you are no longer in the same place, and it relieves the individual you are notifying of any excuses or ignorance.

Finally, you quit. You stop doing what you've been doing and you start doing what you said you were going to do. This is what it comes down to: there needs to be a noticeable, unwavering change in the way you handle those relationships now. This will free you and give us the reinforcement we need to dive all in with you. When you trust us to take care of you and support you, it builds us up as men. When you accompany that with your actions, you have set in motion the steps that will give you everything you need in one person. Now that's what I call a Dream Job.

Friendly Fire

These are your home girls, your homeboys, your BFF's; the people in your daily circle who you call your "friends." As the saying goes, "birds of a feather flock together," and that is somewhat accurate. Even though you and the people you hang with may not be exactly alike, when you're in the same group of friends, they're going to influence who you are and vice versa. Even if they don't influence who you are, they can influence who you're perceived to be. Because of that fact, be careful of the impression your friends give of you. In addition to the perception we receive from your friends, a more important aspect is the actual reality of who and what they are to you, as well as who you are when you're with them. Let's discuss a few of these friend associations.

The Homeboy (a.k.a. the male "bestie") – This is a contradictory topic for me because I don't like the animosity I receive from the guys my close female friends date. At the same time, I do pay close attention to the relationships that girls I date keep with guys who are their so-called "friends." I know it's crazy right? The other side of this coin is that a lot of females are skeptical of the purity of a relationship their man keeps with another woman. No matter how you slice it, it's a touchy **subject**, but here's what needs to take place to conquer it. The key words when dealing with cross gender friendships when you're in a relationship are consideration and communication.

Consideration is simply that, considering how your actions make the other person feel. It's not about how you think they should feel it's about how they actually feel. Just because something doesn't bother you, doesn't mean it's right. When I was in college, a lot of my close female friends who lived on campus would stay at my apartment off campus because it was the party spot. We were all from the same city, we looked out for each other, and our overnight stays were just platonic sleepovers. However, when one of them got a man, they would get grilled and drilled about all the time they spent with the "fellas." Being young and in college, many of my female friends rebelled against their new mates wanting them to withdraw from hanging out with lifelong friends. In all honesty, you should trust whomever you're with and not try to control what they do or who they do it with; as the willing participant of a relationship, you should be willing to do a little adjusting from what you're used to. The fact of the matter is, when you agreed to be someone's significant other, or are trying to get to a level of exclusivity, your relationship status isn't the only thing that changes, so do your obligations. In all fairness, a woman in a relationship, shouldn't be sleeping over at another man's house – friend or not – so just use good judgment.

Communication in this particular instance is all about informing the person you're dating about the nature of this relationship: its origin, history, and future or lack thereof. My closest friend is a female and she makes it a habit to tell her would-be mates about "Donald" in the beginning. Our friendship is not going anywhere and she feels it's only fair to let them know that she spends time, communicates on the regular, and is very close to a person of the opposite sex. She does this to waive any suspicion, and as a mutual respect infomercial for sometimes overly-egotistical males. As a fellow ego driven mammal, I purposely back off in our interactions to allow her potential relationship to grow free from any unnecessary distractions. Unfortunately, all the mention of me ever does is put a bull's-eye on my back and leads these guys to try and get "Donald" out of the picture. This in turn backfires, and they end up on the list of I-hate-your- homeboy exes.

The reason for telling you that story is so you realize that men don't trust other men, just as women don't trust other women. Even the most secure man still will have *I wonder…* thoughts or questions pop in his head from time to time about you and your male friend. There is no clear cut solution to this; just make the male-friend relationship known and its status clear, and hope for the best. If your value is known, a real man will trust you and endure the occasional inconvenience of insecurity produced by your male friends, and therefore obtain you in the process. As in all forms of communication, it's a two way street; allow us the opportunity to comment on how we feel about your male relationships honestly. A lot of times we won't admit to how we really feel, so as not to seem jealous or insecure, and in that case, then that's on us. If by chance we do admit to not liking or trusting a person, don't beat us up with a defensive rebuttal. Relax and just talk it out to a peaceful resolve, because at the end of the day you are trying to make us your men.

Now if you think your male friends caused you to work harder in a relationship, then you better lace up your boots to deal with all the emotional up and downs a female bond can provide. Now let it be known, there is no stronger bond between individuals who do not share the same bloodline than that of female friends. Women are empowered times ten through their connection with their "Girls." You will seldom see a woman out in a social environment without her crew. These women vary by age, background, and complexion, but when they get together they become one cohesive group, for better or worse. There are women out there who don't have female friends, for whatever reasons, and there are women who just can't stand other women, or other women can't stand them to the point that they honestly don't have female friends. I can't discuss these women because I'm telling you how guys think, not women. So to those who ride solo, good luck and God bless; we'll talk in the next chapter. For the rest of you, here is the deal on how your girls affect us as men when we are trying to build something with you.

As I mentioned before, women come in packs and they come in many different flavors. These flavors may not always leave the best taste in our mouths, but the right flavor can be that extra seasoning to get me and you to where we want to be. If you want to know if your girls help or hinder your love life, then identify their flavor. Yeah, you know me by now; it's going to be funny.

The Cherry – this is the girl in your crew that's always nice and positive. She's sweet. She doesn't do drama; she just loves her girls and loves hanging out with them. In reference to us men, she's the one who believes in romance and true love. She has dreams of weddings and engagement parties and long-term blissful relationships. From a man's perspective, we like her. She keeps you thinking about us in a positive light and keeps you emotionally stirred up. Honestly though, the positive input from this pit-less cherry makes our job easier and that's why we like her around. She's our cheerleader and we enjoy having her on our team. She's the one that's going to encourage you to forgive us during our mess-ups and the one that's going to run off any outsiders trying to get to you. All hail the Cherry! The only time we don't like the Cherry is when she gets anxious to plan a wedding and starts asking you what's taking so long to get hitched, then we start looking to can the Cherry. However, for the most part, we love the positivity she brings and we will almost always befriend her as a friend-in-law first. Always keep people in you circle that have good things to say.

A step down from the cherry is **The Apple**. This is the girl in your crew who plays by the book. She's not into the mess, but she's not really into all the fireworks either. She's not overly sweet, but she's not bitter, she's just neutral. This female is not persuaded one way or the other; she just tells the truth and is fair about it. She's not really into your business when it comes to relationships or anything else and for us that's healthy just like an apple. These type friends we appreciate, because they allow you to make up your own mind about your relationship and the decisions made inside of it.

As you can see, the first two are good flavors, but in every bag of jelly beans there's a color you don't like. In relationships, the female friend that we can't stand is **The Lemon**. You know who she is, don't you? The woman that's just sour and bitter because of her history with men, or the absence of a history with men. She is the friend who always has something negative to say. She's the friend who always heard this and that about us. She's the one who knows the momma's/daughter/sister/baby cousin/co-worker that we used to mess with. To keep it clear and simple, we can't stand her. Be careful of this citrus delight, because her motivation is not your wellbeing, she's just on her normal rampage. When we as men get exposed to this person, we will run. We don't like all the drama and shenanigans this person provides and we will sacrifice our friendship with you to avoid it. If you desire to build a relationship, avoid the opinions of the Lemon.

Now of course, there are some women who fall somewhere in the middle. These are the women I like to call **The Strawberry**. This particular friend is confusing, because she's known to be sweet, but for whatever reason she has a bitter edge to her at times. Sometimes she thinks that we are great for you, other times she thinks you should see other people. The sad part about the Strawberry is that she means what she says in either case. We tend to keep the strawberry at a medium distance; not too far to offend her and get on her bad side, but not so close as to get too comfortable with her. The Strawberry tends to pull mixed emotions out of you, and men don't like an emotionally unstable woman. It's too much of a headache.

One more point I would like to make about your female friends is the existence of the BFF (Best Female Friend or Best Friend Forever). This is the girl that has that major connection with you. The one who has cried, lied, and damn near died with you. The good thing about her is the fact that she got your back. That's wonderful! What I want to discuss is that particular BFF that you have supported through all her bad relationships, who you now turn to for advice on your own relationship. She can be the right person to have in your corner, but there is a personality trait I've discovered that kills any potential relationships you may have. It's the Emotional Lesbian. Yes, you heard me correctly; your BFF could be an Emotional Lesbian.

What is an Emotional Lesbian? This is a friend that first of all, really loves you. Secondly, she has been hurt by so many men, that she just doesn't trust or love the same. Because of that, she turns to you for her emotional support. She's able to deal with her issues because you put happiness in a place where there would otherwise be hurt. Basically, emotionally you're her man, or her emotional mate. The confusion comes in for men when we start to gain more of your time and attention and she feels like you're emotionally cheating on her. You become less available for her and that bothers her, so she becomes difficult and a burden to us. Seeing you happy that way, stirs up the reality that she still isn't, and the person she's been in a subliminal relationship with (you), is stepping out on her in her face. To keep your relationship with us on good terms, avoid this emotional love triangle. Emotional Lesbian. Yeah, put that on a T-shirt.

Chapter Four

MONEY MATTERS

There's an old saying that says, "Put your money where your mouth is," which basically means that if you're confident about something, or committed to something, you'll use or risk your money to back it. When it comes to men and our money, we don't even like to do that. If we spend our money on you, that's making a very big statement. Most men work very hard for their money, but even the ones that don't work hard for it, want to hold on to it just the same. The first thing you have to understand is that a man feels pressure to make money. We are looked upon as failures by society if we're broke. Broke men are not respected, not taken seriously, and not afforded the same privileges. Therefore, we're all about our paper. When dating us, or being in a relationship with us, avoid messing up our money.

Granted, some guys are just lazy, unmotivated, and comfortable with being broke. I can't even pretend to understand that mindset, so you'll have to read the book they'll never write to find out why. As for men like me, we are blue collar, white collar, bill paying, nine-to-five, ten-to-six, blood, sweat, and tear go-getters. Some of us are in the corporate world, some of us are on street corners, but we're out there getting it just the same. When it comes to our females, we know it downright turns you on to see a man bring home the bacon. It was put inside us by God himself to be the provider, and no matter how much money you as a female may make, we still like to be considered the breadwinners. I emphasize this so strongly to say that when we pay your bills or use our money to shower you, it's a direct indication that we have included you in our lives. Even if we don't say all the mushy stuff like you would like, when we take our prized possession (money) and apply it to you, we have made a statement just as sentimental as any "I Love You. Knowing that, there are two things you need to remember.

Number One: Don't be a distraction. Put simply, if we have to work or hustle, we don't need you complaining about us being out late or not having enough time for you. I do believe "quality time" is important, but if you know we're working or grinding, then allow us the space and freedom to do so. If we were to lie around on your couch all day and didn't work, we would be available for you whenever you want, but you wouldn't want us then would you? We do need balance, but I would warn against getting in the way of our moneymaking. Ultimately, our pursuit of money is not a vain effort of repetition, there is always a goal in mind. Whether it be to put a down payment on a much needed vehicle, stack up some nest egg money, purchase our kid's school clothes, or put you in that big house you deserve, we have a plan and a purpose. We have a plan that has a follow-up plan behind it, which has a follow-up plan behind that, and so on. What you have to understand is that we are rational beings with continuous goals set to help us get ahead and stay well above water.

<u>Number Two</u>: Don't be a liability. We are not stupid. We know what your needs are for the most part. Anything we don't know, make it known and allow us to deal with it in our own time. Men don't like to feel pressured when it comes to money issues. Just because we don't talk about a money issue, doesn't mean we forgot it. We're just trying to avoid the stress caused by talking about it over and over every day. Avoid being a liability to us by budgeting yourself and not overloading us with financial obligations until we are in a position to voluntarily take on more responsibility. Remember, we are not married. If I have kids to see about, bills of my own to pay, and things I want to accomplish, I don't want the "girlfriend bill" added on to my plate. As a man I want to get to the point where I can say, "I Got You," but my rational way of thinking makes me have to put that a few places down on my priority list. It's not because you're not special enough, it's just that relationships are a luxury and my bills are a necessity. Basically, you're getting whatever we have available to give, but when we care for you, we do what it takes to be able to give you more. Just be patient with us, and appreciate what we do have to offer.

We love a woman that's down with us. That builds a desire in us to want to offer her everything. If your financial needs in a man aren't being met, don't degrade him, just politely leave him alone; you'll both be better off. But to those who are down when we're pinching pennies, we are going to gladly cherish you when we're rolling in the dollars. Now in all fairness, a man shouldn't approach you or involve you in a relationship until he has himself together. He needs to have stability, and have a few things in place to bring to the table, and most guys won't be bothered with a relationship until they do. It can be embarrassing to us to not have our finances straight. What happens is that the nurturing side of a woman sees a man trying to get it together; she's smitten by his drive and determination, and she wants to help him however she can. That's fine, but you should make those efforts with caution and the understanding that getting ourselves together is the main focus during this period. Your voluntary acts of assistance are appreciated, but they don't change a whole lot about that situation. If you ladies really need a sufficient amount of attention or dedication, make your interest and intentions known and then allow us to address them if at all possible. It will help us to avoid feeling obligated, and you to avoid feeling unfulfilled.

At the end of the day, money is important and you have to have it to survive. No one wants to be broke, and the lack of money can put a tremendous strain on a relationship, especially in couples who are not as spiritually bonded as others. The money issue is one of the highest contributing factors to divorce, and I can see how. Don't get it twisted though; if you make each other the focus and have good priorities when it comes to finances, you'll realize that the true value in your relationship isn't measured in dollars and cents.

I'm not completely letting the guys off the hook. One of the most important things to a woman is stability, so don't underestimate the importance of being on top of your business. A man shouldn't be judged by his financial status, but he shouldn't be excused from it either. Secure a stable job, get educated on a trade, lock down a career, take up a side hustle, kickoff that business idea. Do what you have to do to prove to your woman you are both worthy of such a treasure, and stable enough to maintain it. If you're going to put your money where your mouth is, then also put money where your heart is.

Chapter Five

IT'S A DATE

I've come to believe that dating is a lost art. It's been transformed into several different spinoffs, but the traditional method of dating either doesn't work or doesn't exist. I think the reason is that most people don't know what dating really is, or they've mistaken dating as courting. There is a difference. Courting is when you're taking someone you've determined you want to build something more with, on dates. Dating is when you're going out with someone to determine if they're worth courting. Sometimes dating is just going out for the sole purpose of going out. Sometimes you want to go eat dinner and go to a movie, and you want a nice accompaniment and that's all. As a male, there are certain things that just work out better with a female partner. Dinners at upscale restaurants, jazz concerts, and Julia Roberts' movies all tend to be non-male bonding events. The reason I found this topic worthy of its own chapter is because the dating process is a key form of communication in the relationship building process. It's the stage when most of your conversations, interactions, and connections take place.

Confusion or misinterpretation during this phase can be detrimental to the continuance of the friendship, if there even will be a friendship in the future. If you would allow me, I would like to share with you how to read our actions when it comes to dating, questions you need to ask, and issues that women create during this stage. In addition to that, I'll also explain why everyone should approach dating as a sport and not an interview. Sound interesting? Let's go!

I'm sure you have heard the phrase, "You never get a second chance to make a first impression." That's true, and that's the thought process guys operate under when we take a woman on that first date. It's our "sales pitch," that tries to convince you ladies to buy into what we're selling….ourselves. For some of us, that first date is like another day in the office. For others, it's like an interview for a job you feel you're not qualified for. Either way, it's something we all must go through to break the ice and begin the "getting to know each other" process. What you have to remember about dating is that some play it like chess and some play it like checkers. Once you know what game you're playing, you'll be better equipped to handle dating. So what's the difference between chess and checkers? I'm glad you asked.

Chess is a game of strategy. It's planned, thought out, and manipulated, with the intent of acquisition of the Queen. When a guy is a chess player, he's going to cater to your likes, account for your dispositions, and do whatever you want to do. Everything will be all about you, even to the point that he will transform his likes, wants, and desires to what you need them to be. The goal of a chess player is to make everything comfortable for you and provide everything you need, so you have nothing missing and no justification to look for anything elsewhere. A woman that is happy and comfortable will not leave that comfort level to explore something that is unproven. Once a chess player has figured out your favorite restaurants, your preference of flowers, you're most interesting topics of conversation, and your list of things not to do: checkmate. At that point, he has positioned you to concede to his pursuit of you and hopefully his intentions were pure. Some chess players play for keeps, some play for sex and/or money. Sad but true.

On the other hand, the checkers player is a little different. Checkers is a game of fun. You move, I move. I get some of your checkers, you get some of mine. If I lose a round, no big deal, let's play again. It's not that serious. It's all about having a good time. When a guy is a checkers player, he desires to interact with you and receive a certain level of pleasure and excitement. He doesn't have a hidden agenda or ulterior motive, and probably hasn't thought passed the current date. For women, a checkers player is good for you, even if you may not think so. Checkers players appreciate your company and truly desire just having a good time with you. They can end up being some of the best friends you'll ever make. Sometimes a woman is dating with the intent of building something more and a checkers player doesn't always give off those signals. Checkers players are all about fun, while women tend to date hoping to eventually get down to business. Women want to know, "Where is this going?" That's a legitimate concern, but with the checkers player, relationships are going to be more of a natural transition over time.

Chess players create the vision of the anticipated ending and work backwards. Checkers players honestly don't know where things are going to end up. So when you venture into the world of dating, and you you're sitting across the table from each other look down and see if there are pawns, bishops, and knights or just a bunch of red and black chips.

Now that you understand our approach to dating, how do you identify which game we're playing? That's easy, you just ask. It's called conversation. Ask us what our short and long term goals are. If we have plans of having a family and raising kids, then you know a relationship is probably in our up-and-coming plans. If we have plans to go to medical school, climb Mount Everest, or go on tour with Lady Gaga, then we're probably not looking for anything serious right now, and you can react accordingly. Also, ask us about our past relationships. We are creatures of habit and we tend to trend, so if my last three relationships have ended peacefully and I'm cool with my exes, then I'm probably a good guy and just haven't found the right one yet. If my last three relationships have ended up in five divorces, don't bother doing the math, just run.

In case you lost your place in the book, I want to let you know that this chapter is on dating not commitment, marriage, or sex. As men, we hate when women attach dating to those things. Those things are often the result of dating, but they are not a guaranteed end result. The issue that women create a lot of times is that all those things get mixed up in the realm of dating. I'll go into greater detail in the chapters to follow, but I would like to briefly say this: even if we are going on a date every other day, the only meaning you can take is that I like your company. Anything more than that is an assumption. Don't take frequent dating as commitment. Don't take frequent dating as an obligation to have sex. Don't take frequent dating as a request or a desire to be married.

On the flip side, some guys think you owe them something or you're their "girl" when you're dating. In that situation, make your status and your intentions very clear. If the guy can't respect where you are, chunk him the deuces. One point I want to stress about dating is that it's not a form of commitment unless you have had a conversation and agreed to date each other exclusively. Otherwise, the only thing you're committing to is being somewhere at a certain time. So if someone you're going out with goes out with someone else, that's totally fine. Don't read too much into that, it's actually healthy.

Earlier I stated that you should approach dating as a sport and not an interview, and I know that those of you who think so far ahead cringed at the way that sounded. You're the ones who need to hear that the most. True enough, when you're dating, you're attempting to learn someone. You want to find out who they are, what they're about, and what their motives, agendas, and goals are. You want to know what you can do for each other, if anything, very much like an interview. However, when you perform an interview, you are looking to hire someone for a position you need filled. Your company has a vacancy that's not allowing it to function at one hundred percent capacity and you need to put the best possible applicant in that spot. In relationships you should never operate out of need. You need to already be at one hundred percent efficiency on your own and any outsider that you bring into your life is just a bonus, not a necessity. I always tell people: "Before you start looking for a relationship, you need to already be happy, and whoever comes into your life should make you happ*ier*. That way if it doesn't work out, when they leave, you won't be as happy, but you'll still be happy." That's crucial when dating because it keeps you from sitting across the table from someone hoping their background check will come back clean so you can hire them as your husband. When you do that, you're operating out of a need and you have an expectation. When you have an expectation which most times the man has no clue about, it sets you up for a letdown.

If that man doesn't walk the way you want him to walk, or say what you think he should say, you can't even enjoy what could otherwise be good company and fun times with a nice person. Why is that? It's because a grown woman has an idea in her mind of what her husband looks like, sounds like, acts like, smells like, dresses like, etc. They have the ending of the play written before the introduction, and they spend all their time and effort trying to write a story that matches their preset ending. This almost always ends in failure. It's okay to have a goal, but it's dangerous to have an obsession. Allow some room in your goals for adjustments, or even a plan b, c, & d. Now I understand that the guy that you've been dating is the right complexion, has the same religious beliefs, and he's over six feet tall, but he's probably just as uninterested in being someone's man as the short, atheist brother you were talking to before him. What you have to understand about men is that we're not like you. While a woman thinks she knows what her husband is going to be like, men have fewer requirements and more short term goals. Basically, if you're pretty, shapely, and giving us the time of day, we're in. Honestly, you can just be one of those things and you got us. Why? Because we're not dating out of need, we're dating because we just want to. I want to see the new Madea movie, and my momma already saw it, so what are you doing Thursday? That's the gist of it. The problem is that women build an emotional connection quickly because time spent together is perceived as quality time. For most men, time spent together is either a timely ego boost, or an expense/investment with an optimistic/anticipated return. Sounds shallow? Well, yeah.

To all my female friends out there, listen up. You are all beautiful and worthy of having everything your heart desires, and anyone who is blessed to receive your time, attention, affection, and love is damn lucky. I mean that from the bottom of my heart. However, outside of your plans, God has a plan too, and his plan is a lot more detailed and foolproof than yours. What or who he has for you will come in his designated time. In the meantime, loosen up. Go to that poetry recital, take that invitation for the picnic in the park, and let the guy at work treat you to a day at the museum. Have some fun. It's on your terms and at your pace, and no one can judge you. Give someone a chance to spoil you. Give someone a chance to earn your friendship. Besides, in this economy, who wants to pay ten dollars for their own movie ticket?

Chapter Six

DO YOU UNDERSTAND

the Words that are Coming out of my Mouth?

Wkhen I was in fifth grade, I got my first love note. It simply read:

I like you. Do you like me?

Yes ☐

No ☐

Maybe So ☐

It was direct and to the point. It didn't leave much to the imagination. It didn't offer much opportunity for misunderstanding or confusion. Basically, I'm feeling you, is it reciprocated? You make a determination and decision, check the appropriate box, and you are officially hitched. *Sigh.* Life was so simpler then. Fast forward about twenty-five years, and issue the same letter, and this is what you'll get:

- "So, could you please define *like.*"

- "Why do you like me?"

- "Didn't you just come out of a 'like' situation with someone else a few months ago?"

- "You know, I've been hurt bad, and I don't know if I can like again."

What? I mean come on, does it require all that? Well, in all actuality, it does. When you're a kid, you don't have any responsibility other than not leaving your skateboard in the driveway. There is no one that will be affected by your decision to be in a "relationship" other than the fourth grade boy she left for you. In an adult's world, everything about you will affect everything about me at some point. At thirty, thirty-five, forty, and forty-five years old; I don't have the time to not have clarity about a person's intentions, motives, or requirements. I need both of us to be on the same page. How do we achieve this clear understanding of each other? Communication.

Communication is broken down into four forms.

1. What you say,

2. What you don't say,

3. What you do,

4. What you don't do.

Simple? Okay, let's discuss it…let's communicate

What You Say

One of my favorite scriptures is: "Death and life are in the power of the tongue: and they that love it shall eat the fruit thereof" (Proverbs 18:21). This scripture is so powerful to me because it lets you know that with God, you can literally just speak something and it sets things in motion to make it happen. Unfortunately, that principle applies to negative speaking just as much as positive speaking. In relationships, it's the same principle. What you speak into it will set things in motion to give you a negative or positive outcome. If you constantly tell me how great I am, whether I initially believe it or not, at some point I'm going to buy into your way of thinking. If you tell me how much you love me, before your actions ever catch up to your words, I'm going to accept your claims of endearment as truth. What your positive words are doing, is setting a healthy environment that allows those things you're hoping for to grow into fruition. That's why it's crucial to always find a way to communicate as civil, respectful, and encouraging as possible.

As men, we have a lot of pride and big egos that dictate how we receive and respond to your words. My experience with women has also taught me to realize, it's not just what you say, but how you say it. If you're cutting your eyes, rolling your neck, and talking loud when you tell me something, you have totally missed me. If you're calm, and your words are soft and sweet, you're probably going to get whatever you want. Not only that, we aren't always the best at figuring out what you need or want, so in addition to being nice when communicating with us, be clear. A lot of times, women put us through a test to see how well we know them.

A woman will say, "Go to the store and get me a bag of Doritos." The man will proceed to the store, pick up a bag of Doritos and return home. When he gets home, the woman will say, "You got regular Doritos, you know I only eat Cool Ranch. You got this big old bag of Doritos too, I can't eat all that. You didn't get me anything to drink either?" The man is standing there like, what? The disconnection is that the man heard a request for a bag of chips, but in the woman's mind, she wanted to be catered to by someone who knew her inside and out. Even though it's a humble desire to want a man that knows what you mean despite what you actually say, you still have the responsibility to groom your man into that psychic being through communication and experience over time.

In my most recent relationship, my ex always wanted a bottle of Coca-Cola, but she had to have a cup of ice to go along with it. Under no circumstances should I purchase one for her without the other. That was easy to remember because she instilled that in my head out of the gate. She verbally communicated to me, I like this, this way, and will be upset if I don't receive it that way every time. Two years later, and I was still doing the same thing. That's effective communication. A woman likes nothing more than for a guy to pay enough attention to her to learn her, and we should. Until we get that process down though, help us out with a little instruction. We will both be happier in the end.

Another major point about what you say in a relationship is for you to clarify where we are and where we're going in this relationship. Although a lot of people don't like to admit it, and I'm not justifying it, some relationships are not sought after with the intent of finding a spouse. Some relationships people engage in are for financial, sexual, or some other kind of fringe benefit. The importance of communication in these situations is to make sure both parties are aware of the nature of the relationship. Most times guys are tagged with the reputation of seeking out these superficial relationships, and are often accused of pretending to be interested in more, but wanting less. However, life has taught me that women are equally responsible for these benefits based agreements. In either case, you want to be up-front, clear, and direct about your desires and intentions. Omission of all the facts is the same as lying about them. Ladies, if you're looking for a cash-for-attention exchange, tell a man that in the beginning, and let him determine if he wants that. If you're interested in finding a husband by next summer, please communicate that as well. When the person you're with knows what your intentions are, they can determine whether or not to continue. On occasion, some people will still move forward, and pretend to be what you want for their own benefit. Those people are trifling, and we all get exposed to and hurt by these people. It's going to happen. However, don't be discouraged, there are a lot of good, honest, trustworthy people out there who will respect and heed your wishes. Just remember, the first step to having your wishes granted, is to request the wish in the first place.

And by the way, I previously mentioned the power of the words you speak. Here's a short list of phrases you need to do away with:

- "All men are dogs;"
- "A good man is hard to find;"
- "I'm going to be single my whole life;"
- "I won't ever be happy;"
- "Can't no man can handle me;"
- "I won't change for anybody;"
- Insert your own here.

What You Don't Say

One of my favorite comic books/cartoons/movies is X-Men, and the leader of the X-Men is Professor Charles Xavier. Professor Xavier has the power to read and control your mind. He knows exactly what you're thinking. He can even read your memories and review your history, background, and past experiences. Without you saying one word, the Professor gets precise and detailed information about you straight from the source. Can you imagine having that kind of power? Can you imagine being able to fully understand a person's mindset? Wow! How convenient! But then I realized something, even Professor Xavier is single. If he can read your mind and can't maintain a relationship, then the rest of us are in for a long day.

In all seriousness, you can search the world over and you will not find a mind reader; so you're actually going to have to open your mouth and speak. We are not comic book characters with super powers. We are human beings who learn through life's lessons and experiences. Anything I want to be good at in life, from business to romance, I need to have been instructed on how to do it, or have experienced it enough times to know how it works. In a relationship, you need to teach me how to be your mate. I need you to actually say, "I don't like this," "I prefer this," "I would like this to happen this way." I'm not saying that some preferences are not just common sense, but if you communicate it, then you remove the possible confusion associated with assumptions. What you have to realize is that anyone that cares about you desires to make you happy and meet your needs. Who would purposely not give you what you're looking for? The problem is that a lot of you have been taken advantage of by divulging too much info. A lot of you have just been so hurt by past men, that to get with you becomes an immense challenge. It's like a Rubik's Cube. Yes, there is a solution to this puzzle, but it's not easily obtained. You want men to figure you out and prove our worth to you, to offset any insecurity you have towards us. The ones before us put your emotions in jeopardy, now you're looking for a Superman to come and save your heart from danger, instead of just letting a regular guy do the normal things that will be sufficient enough to please you. You feel like you can't give us too much ammunition that we may turn around and fire back at you later. However, you can't hold me liable for the damage caused by someone else. What you can do, is tell me where it hurts and help me place a bandage on the wound. I know it's not easy, but there's no way around it. Communicating your needs, especially if we're asking you what they are, is the only way to ensure that they're met.

Oh, but ladies, don't think for one second that men are exempt from this closed mouth syndrome, because we become mute when it comes to saying how things make us feel emotionally. We tend to be too prideful when it comes to admitting we're uncomfortable with something, and we're too embarrassed to say when something actually makes us feel good. You do have some men that are emotional and in touch with their feelings, but most of us want to keep you with the strong, chest out, head high image you have of us. From our pee wee league football coach, to our drunken uncle at the family reunion, we're taught to be strong. However, as we grow older and wiser, we learn that it takes a whole lot more strength to admit a weakness, than to endure the pain caused by it. When you're dating us, don't settle for no response. We really do want to tell you how we feel, but we're not the best at this part of the relationship process.

I've learned to be open emotionally by making up in my mind that I don't care what other people think or say. I've become comfortable in expressing myself by becoming secure in myself. If I feel a certain way, it's just how I feel, and I don't need to front. If you want your mate to get to that point, assist him by not making him feel lesser when it's obvious he has an issue with something. Offer things about yourself more willingly, and let him know you're in this together. The biggest thing is, don't ever give negativity in response to honesty. If he musters up enough courage to tell you the truth, embrace the fact he loves you enough to be honest, and don't lash out if it's the truth about something that not exactly favorable. If you ask me if I like your new hairdo, and I really don't, I'd rather say no now and deal with it once, than to have to keep seeing that same ugly finger wave-freeze-Mohawk combination. Then a year later, when I just can't take it anymore, when it comes out I really don't like it, you're going to be even more upset, and I would have suffered through a whole year of trying to hide you from the public. I understand you're trying to look good for me, but if it's truly for me, shouldn't it be what I like?

For example: I went on a first date with a girl, and I took her out to a dinner and a movie. In my mind, I thought I was Mr. Casa Nova, and I had this dating thing down. When we met up, in an effort to impress her, I wanted to be a take charge guy. I had the restaurant picked out, the movie picked out, and all the details. What my ignorant self didn't realize is that it's not about what I *think* she likes. I could've communicated with her and I would have *known* what she likes. I mean, who knows what she likes better than she does? It's like reading the owner's manual for a Chevy to figure out how to operate a BMW. In my efforts, I actually passed up one of her favorite restaurants to go to a restaurant she didn't really care for. I also took her to a movie when she was actually a little tired and would've preferred to just cuddle up with me somewhere. I was such a loser. The upside is that she eventually corrected me on the error of my ways and I learned a valuable lesson that the women after her benefited from. Now women think I'm so in touch with their needs, and I actually am, but I had to be taught that. It had to be communicated to me. Oh by the way, to my Texas homies: if you're not sure, go with Papadeaux's. Trust me on this one.

What You Do

I'm sure you've all heard the old adage: "Actions speak louder than words," which means what you actually do carries a lot more weight than what you say you will do. Ideas, concepts, and dreams are seeded in the spirit, conceived in the mind, spoken in the mouth, and lay dormant until action is taken to bring it to life. If you have been seeded to be someone's mate, and you have visualized your wedding day in your head, and you have claimed your spouse verbally, why are your actions contrary to that? If you know you want Prince Charming, why are you still dating the Court Jester? I've read lonely, late night posts on Facebook where women say, "I can't wait till I'm lying next to the man of my dreams." Then they close their laptop, and text that same old knucklehead they've been messing with for the past five years to come by when he leaves the club–if he's not with his girlfriend tonight. *Really*? It's time you ladies take some accountability for your situation. If you say you want to be a nurse, but you never enroll in nursing school, you're not going to be a nurse. If you say you want a good man, but you never engage in a healthy relationship, you're not going to get that either. I'm tired of hearing about what men don't do. You can't control what another person does. What you can control is what you do, and a lot of you are not doing your part.

I consider myself a good man, and I don't want just anybody. I've busted my butt to be able to be a supportive, intelligent, stable, spiritual, mature man. I bring a lot to the table and have a lot to offer. Why should I settle for less? I was born in 1975 and grew up as a young black man in the 80s, 90s, and 2000s, where I wasn't handed anything. Yet I offer no excuses or complaints about what's fair or what I'm owed. Life isn't fair, and your decisions and choices will determine where you end up. Before you engage in an unprotected sexual relationship with the deadbeat dude from around the corner – think again. Before you get a tattoo on your neck – think again. Before you go to the club every weekend with your "goods" hanging out – think again. Before you take that abusive lover back – think again. Before you smoke weed or get pissy drunk at the party – think again. Before you lay down with every guy in the neighborhood to feel accepted – think again. Before you put that blue weave in your hair with those super long nails, and seventeen earrings in your ear – think again. Before you go out with "them girls," that curse and act crazy in public – think again. By no means am I judging anyone. People are who they are. I love everybody, and I honestly believe you can overcome any mistake you may have made in the past. All I'm saying is, what you put out there is what you get back.

I have to be real with you in order to help you. If you advertise ghetto, I might entertain you for some kind of short term benefit, but do you really think I see my bride matching her weave with her bridesmaid's gown? Uh, no. The only way that appeals to me is if my mindset is in the same place, and in that case God help us both. Do you think I want to be the guy that's married to the girl the entire neighborhood has been with? Do you think I want my political campaign smeared because of your weed habit? Do you think I should be restricted because of your choices? If I love you, I'm willing to make some sacrifices, but some things I just shouldn't have to deal with. How would you feel if I couldn't support you because I couldn't get a job? How would you feel if I had seven baby mommas? How would you feel if I had "thug life" tattooed on my forehead? Honestly? My point is, try to make a conscious decision to be the best you, so that you are capable of acquiring the best for you. You are wonderfully made and God created you for greatness, so don't settle for less than that.

What You Don't Do

I remember going to a conference at my kid's school, and the teacher told me that my daughter wasn't turning in her assignments. When my daughter came into the room, I asked her what the problem was, and she said, "I didn't do anything." I said, "That's why we're here." Funny story, but it's true in relationships. What you fail to do could be just as damaging as actually doing something wrong. I know a lot of women who don't go out, don't give out their number, don't date, and aren't interested in making new friends. That's all fine and dandy, but those same women are the ones who say they can't find a nice man to share their life with. I've never claimed to be a relationship guru, but you just might be a little bit isolated. Remember, this chapter is about communication, and that requires at least two people to function properly. Even if we actually get past the introduction stage, do you actually talk, laugh, and discuss current events, share likes and dislikes? Do you just sit there and dissect everything that you don't like? A lot of women want to be built up in a relationship, and you deserve it, but are you helping to build up the person that's helping build up you. Are you encouraging us? Are you connecting with us? Are you actively involved, or are you just waiting for us to come in and make this perfect all on our own? If you truly want a good relationship, you have to make some effort.

Now for those of you in a relationship, there are certain things that we as men expect. You have to remember that we are barbaric, like cavemen with lion-type pride, and we are encouraged and motivated by your actions. If you're not the type of girl to let us know we are doing a good job of being your man, we are going to question our place and probably let it go. If you are the type of girl that can't let a man take the lead, at least sometimes, it's going to cause a rift in the relationship. We are leaders, and no woman wants a weakling, so allow us the opportunity to lead. If you never confirm the fact that you are exclusively ours because you just don't feel it needs to be said, we are going to think we are not the only one and hold back on how much we give you of ourselves. I'm not saying it's all the ladies fault. A lot of times men are uncomfortable or insecure in a relationship, and we can become overbearing in an effort to receive validation from you. In those cases, we don't create an environment conducive to allowing you to do those previously stated things. Sometimes we fish for compliments or try so hard to be dominant in the relationship that we shut you down, and ultimately run you away. When we go off on that path, give us a nudge and tell us to slow down and calm down. Point out to us that it doesn't require all that, because honestly enough, what you don't do could be a direct result of what we don't allow you to do.

One last point, which is a major point when we're talking about what you don't do, is the dreaded act of letting go. We all have past hurts, disappointments, and experiences that have left us with scars, fears, and dispositions. We take those past negatives and hold them as painful truths and vow never to be exposed to those moments of vulnerability and weakness again. Our attitude is: "I will never be hurt that way again," and what one or two people have done becomes what every person is trying to do. *Our past experiences become a tangible threat in our present, and an anticipated ending in our future.* We walk around hesitant, pessimistic, and even bitter when it comes to being in a relationship. We don't let go and allow someone else to make any progress in their attempt to love us. It's what we refer to as, "putting our guards up," which serves as a false sense of security in relationships. It's a mental barrier that draws an imaginary line in the sand that we dare not cross emotionally or physically. It's really just fear! We're simply afraid. All those things you don't do such as commit, admit you like someone, or even allow someone to do anything nice for you, are by-products of a fear in you that we didn't create. Yes, a real man or woman will help you move past your fears, but ultimately overcoming your fears is your responsibility.

I started this chapter off with a scripture and I think it's only fitting to end it with one: "For God has not given us a Spirit of fear, but of power and of love and of a sound mind" (II Timothy 1:7). Negativity will happen to all of us, especially in the search of the right relationship, but what doesn't kill you will only make you stronger and wiser, so press on. Life is for the living, but living in fear is not living at all. If you find yourself holding back because of the fear of being hurt again, you could be letting the acts of the wrong one for you, hinder your growth with the right one for you. If there's anything you don't do, don't do that.

Chapter Seven

THE "C" WORD

Commitment

Werewolves have silver bullets, vampires have wooden stakes, but if you're looking for a way to finish off a relationship with a man all you have to do is simply mention the word "commitment." You'll have an easier time getting a two-year-old child to Parallel Park an 18-wheeler, than to get a man to commit. For most men, our single lives define us. It's not that we don't like being in relationships, but nothing is more sacred to a man than his freedom. Remember, we mature a lot later in life than women, so in most cases the men you are dealing with are nothing more than grown up boys. We want to hunt, fish, play basketball, watch football, tinker in our woodshops, wax our cars, hook up our sound systems, eat potato chips, hangout in bars, get our hands dirty, listen to our music loud, drink beer, eat pizza, and the list goes on and on and on. We would rather sit around the domino table and talk about women than put in the work to sustain a relationship with one.

We're unconsciously taught that women are acquisitions that we obtain in numbers as proof of our male prowess. These female trophies are catch and release though, and not intended for long term ownership, because of the amount of maintenance they require. To be in a committed relationship requires compromise and sacrifice of a lot of those things we love to do, and we're just not looking forward to the loss of our privileges. Sound shallow yet? Good, because you need to understand that it really is that shallow. Quit watching these relationship experts trying to get some deep, philosophical explanation of why your man won't commit. It's fairly easy to explain. As men, what we like and what we like to do is simple. Give us some sort of a ball, food, and free time and we are good. No worries, no concerns. To initiate, maintain, and grow a relationship is hard. The complexity of a woman is a challenge to the mortal mind of a man. Being committed to, living up to the expectations of, and learning to understand a woman is like attending Harvard for the rest of your life. When I compare eating buffalo wings and watching the New Orleans Saints play to discussing how to better meet your emotional needs; I'm going with Drew Brees every time (And for you ladies who don't know who Drew Brees is, you're just strengthening my argument). Commitment is not just hard work, but its work that we're not sure that we are qualified to do. So now, I'm not only overworked, I'm insecure because I feel inadequate. What part of this situation is supposed to be appealing to me again?

When it comes to basketball, I know I'm good at handling the ball, I'm a great passer, I have a decent jumper, and I actually love doing it. When it comes to being in a committed relationship, most guys don't even know what position they're playing. As men, we love to meet new women, and we enjoy the process of getting to know you. We like to date because we like the attention women give us, but dating affords us the option of being with you or not. Commitment removes the ability, or should I say comfort, to choose. Ladies, are you understanding what I'm saying? Well, before you close up this book, and throw it in the trash, let me offer you a different viewpoint.

Relationships are a gamble, and commitment is like playing all your chips in one hand. Some men are only giving up a few chips at a time, trying to make their money last. Some men are hopping from game to game, trying to see which one they are better at. Some men are just plain greedy, and want as many chips as they can get. Some men are playing with scared money, and only place "safe" bets. After it's all said and done, men aren't trying to "win" in relationships, they're just trying not to lose. From the outside looking in, it seems selfish, immature, and irresponsible, but really it's simply fear. Men come off as big bad wolves, but older women will tell you we're just sheep on steroids.

For every woman who is optimistic about relationships, there are twenty guys who are pessimistic. We don't trust women, mainly because we have a guilty conscious from our own actions. We don't like the sacrifice a relationship requires, mainly because we are too immature to make those life changes that we eventually all will have to make. We don't openly commit, because we are too proud to do anything that shows the world we feel some kind of positive, mushy emotion for a yucky, little girl. Ugh (We're trapped in the third grade emotionally).

I know you're thinking to yourself, "Is he serious?" Yes, I am. My emotional inadequacy and immaturity may come out in different forms: cheating, arguing, excuses for everything, promiscuity, emotionally distant, being controlling, or even overly physical or violent in some cases. However it's presented, it still stems from our poor ability to handle emotions and our fear of failure. Now you kind of feel sorry for us, don't you? Well, thanks! Under no circumstances am I excusing anyone's negative behavior. We are all adults and are to be held liable for our actions. At some point in life you just have to grow up and handle your business, but if you are with someone you care about and you think they are worth the investment, let me show you how to address these issues.

When dealing with a woman, its best to find out why she wants to commit. What's her motivation? Well, with men, if you want commitment, you have to find out why he doesn't want to. You have to get past what it seems like on the surface and get to the root of the problem. Men operate from the brain, not the heart; we are thinkers and vastly imaginative. We are good at coming up with stories and lies to cover up what's really going on. We are simply playing roles. That is why I call us "bad actors." Let's look at what movie your potential mate may be starring in.

Bad Actors

BIG – In this movie, Tom Hanks is a kid that makes a wish to be bigger. He then wakes up the next morning in a grown man's body. By a coincidental turn of events, he gets a job at a toy company designing and approving new designs on toys. Because he is really a kid inside, his fun and youthful nature causes him to excel in this job initially. He gets to play with toys all day, he has money like he's never had before, and he doesn't have any adult supervision. Tom Hanks' character has been thrown into a situation he's never experienced before and it's all fun, fun, fun. The conflict in this movie comes when he's forced to make adult decisions. When he has to engage in things that require responsibility, or when he has to handle and make mature decisions about business and personal relationships, he struggles severely. Even though everyone loves him because of how fun he is, his immaturity in life's serious situations is a handicap he cannot escape. He slowly becomes more and more exposed as a kid trying to make it as an adult in a grown up situation. He eventually goes back to being a kid because he's just not ready for what being an adult calls for.

This is very common in relationships, and is a consistent barrier to reaching your commitment goals. As I stated before, women mature faster than guys. A twenty-seven-year-old woman is equivalent to a thirty-three-year-old man, in a sense of where they are in their life. A twenty-seven-year-old woman is solid on her career goals, the number of children she wants, where she wants to reside, and even where she plans to be in the next twenty years. A twenty-seven-year-old guy barely knows what he wants for breakfast. You see, in a twenty-seven-year-old woman's plans, all those things I named includes room for her husband or the desired lack thereof. She includes a mate in her plans, unless she has decided that she will seek a mate at a later time. However, in a twenty-seven-year-old man's mind, the idea of sharing anything, building anything, or planning anything with a woman has never entered his mind.

What happens here is that women meet men in this stage, and these men are vivacious and full of life. They are fun! They are at their peaks. At that age, they finally have jobs that pay them decent money. They have nicer places and nicer vehicles now, and the world is their oyster. They are finally free from their parent's supervision, and they can whiz you around town, keep you out all night, and bring you to a point of being carefree that you haven't experienced in a long time. He can finally afford some of those toys he's been longing for. The new stereo, the PS3 with all the games, and the trip to Mexico are all within his grasp. This young, vibrant, live-life-to-the-fullest individual seems like the perfect mate for a woman, until it's time to make those non-fun decisions. When the woman wants to have that discussion about where the relationship is going, the man wonders, *why are you trying to spoil all the fun?* When the nature of a woman takes over and she starts needing some form of security and stability, she's going to require the man to make some adult decisions. These are decisions he's going to struggle with, and eventually run from. Just like Tom Hanks' character, the woman enjoys his fun nature, but he is still a kid inside and not capable of making the proper adult decisions she requires of him. Even though his immaturity brings an aspect to the table that initially is inviting to you, it ultimately will be his demise. So how do you fast forward through this movie?

When a man is in this stage, he's not going to want to give up any of his privileges. If you want to avoid being put in this situation, you simply have to spend the time and ask the questions that are going to reveal our maturity. The quickest way to see if a man is in this stage is to try to get him to give up his time or freedoms. Try to add responsibility to his life that will only benefit you. Ask him to wash your car, mow your lawn, babysit, pay some of your bills, or sacrifice some of his male bonding time. The response he gives you will show you where he's at in his life. If you then see the signs, and that's not what you're looking for, then move on. Maybe you can remain friends and revisit the idea of being a couple at a later date. If you are currently in a relationship with this type person, and you want to ride it out, I suggest you compromise in small steps. A man's immaturity can be overcome by his character, and a good woman is still appreciated by a good man. It's just the weight of maintaining her too early in our development that rocks the love boat. And don't think that dating older is an automatic fix, because age does not maturity make. Remember, Tom Hanks became older, but his mind was still young. Many guys are of a certain age biologically, but mentally we are still in the sandbox. You see, girls aren't the only ones that just wanna have fun.

The Negotiator – In this movie, Chris Sapien (played by Kevin Spacey) was chosen by Danny Roman (played by Samuel Jackson) to be the negotiator for a hostage crisis he created because he was a stranger that would play everything by the book. The people in Jackson's circle had betrayed him and he didn't know who to trust. When everything was said and done, Spacey saw that Jackson was really a good person who was forced into this negative situation because his trust in his former friends had been broken and he felt alone. He only trusted himself. Throughout the movie, they went back and forth bargaining for things such as the release of hostages, electricity, information, etc. Each one of them tried to gain an advantage over the other to be in control of the situation. This is a really good movie to watch, but it's not such a pleasant view when you're dating Danny Roman.

In this example, the guy you are dealing with has been hurt by a past relationship. Somewhere down the line, he allowed himself to let go and be in a committed relationship, and the person he trusted turned on him. Whether it was cheating or just calling the relationship off, it left him with a feeling of being alone in the situation. Now, his motivation in relationships is to put himself in a position of control. He wants an advantage. He needs the upper hand in order to feel comfortable, so what he does is negotiate everything in the relationship to his advantage. Have you dated this brother before? The guy who needs everything his way or he's not going forward. This is the guy who keeps you on the phone all night persuading you to give into his demands for attention or sex. Have you negotiated dinner plans, relationship boundaries, and even where you go and what you do with this intense negotiator? Does it seem that after the negotiating is done, he has gotten his way, or you're back at square one? If this is the movie you're trapped in, here's how to write a happy ending.

The first thing is to be a stern negotiator yourself. Don't give into to demands that will cause you to have animosity later. If you are just not comfortable with something, don't agree to it. In the end, if you're unhappy, you'll never make the relationship a happy one. Secondly, earn his trust. We really want our relationships to be healthy ones, but we tread very cautiously in the pursuit of it. Remember, initially you're a stranger and we don't have a reason to trust you, but we don't have a reason not too either. Make those extra little comments of reassurance. Cater to what he's dealing with just a little. If you find him worth it, prove to him that this situation is different. Become his Chris Sapien and he'll know that you are the only chance he's got if he wants to get out of his bad predicament in one piece.

Night of the Living Dead – This is one of my favorite throwback horror flicks. In this classic movie something happens that causes the dead to arise and walk the earth in an attempt to eat and destroy all living things. If you encounter these walking dead, and they bite you, you eventually transform into one of them. After becoming one of them, you too were destined to walk the earth searching for your next victim, looking to consume a living human being. The funny thing about it was that the dead were lifeless monsters, but they recognized each other as zombies, and recognized the living as living, and they literally walked around in packs looking for victims. I found that to be very interesting. So, how does that translate into relationships and commitment?

The evidence of life is growth and transition. From the conception of life, you grow physically, mentally, spiritually, or emotionally every day. Whenever you stop growing and maturing, you are either dead or in the process of dying. Some guys are stuck in the same place and refuse to grow when it comes to relationships and commitments. These are the guys that are forty-years-old playing the same games, living the same life, and doing the same things they did at twenty-one. They have not grown or matured in years. They don't have anything positive going on; they're just looking to see what they can consume in you. They have no desire to change, no desire to grow. They are emotionless shells, basically zombies.

Be very careful if you're involved with a zombie. Remember, they are already dead, so don't think you have the power to bring them back to life. Also remember the rule of the movie: if you encounter one of them, it's very likely they will bite you and slowly transform you into one of them. When you're in a relationship with such a person, you get to a point where you just don't care. You're in that relationship, you're not going anywhere, and you just accept it as it is. Some situations are not as obvious to the eye as being a dead relationship. Sometimes you end up just going through life in a relationship that isn't really bad, but just has no growth. Those relationships are where you remain the "lil' boo," the girlfriend, or even the fiancé forever. Those situations put you in a place where you have peaked in that relationship, and if you are no longer growing or blossoming, you are dead or dying. You yourself have become a zombie and you live out the days of this relationship hoping and looking for some sort of living thing to feed you. You end up feasting on your living friends, jobs, hobbies, or even an outside relationship. You'll be searching for anything that will supplement your dead state.

I referenced earlier how the zombies recognized each other and ran in packs. Well, if you think someone may fit the description, look at their friends to validate that. If they hang out with some zombie-like dudes, they are probably the same way. In this situation, simply avoid the zombies. They move slowly, and they're pretty stupid, so be quick and cunning. Don't fear growth and change in life and relationships. If something is not growing, then its season is over and it needs to be replanted somewhere else. However, if you just insist on riding it out with your zombie, remember the only way to kill them is to shoot them in the head. Translation: you have to change their mindset. You have to upgrade his way of thinking and make him want something better. Luckily, if they have you in their life, they have already begun the process of acquiring the finer things in life.

Chapter Eight
BREAKING UP IS HARD TO DO

Once you've actually gotten a guy to commit to a relationship and you've been together for a while, you may realize that after all the work to establish it, it's not the right situation for you. Well if you have had a cell phone, satellite television, or a Netflix subscription in the past few years, you'll know that getting out of an agreement can be just as hard as getting into one. Men are not the best at handling rejection. Some of us are mature and secure, and recognize the signs of a relationship that isn't just coming together like it's supposed to, but a lot of us think that we are God's personal gift to women and you had better recognize how blessed you are to be in our presence. Those who think they are doing you a favor by being in a relationship together, end up being the main ones you can't seem to get rid of. As I thought about this topic, I wondered: What are the reasons some guys just can't let go of some of these relationships. What are the factors that lead to a guy trying to hurt you verbally, emotionally, or even physically, as a reaction for you simply not wanting to be in a relationship anymore? What are the triggers that make a man act out in a negative way when facing a break up? What is the catalyst that transforms this man you thought you knew into this name calling, idle threatening, text messaging, begging, and pleading individual in your front yard? I think I might have a few explanations of why breaking up is hard to do.

Break Up to Make Up

A Stylistics song inspired this section. The general idea of the chorus is that it's a ridiculous idea to break up just to make up. This reminds me of a classic issue in relationships. The issue I'm referring to is when you are with someone and they progressively treat you badly, but the second you get enough they go into regretful lover mode. When I say treat you badly, I'm referring to the negative comments, complaining, and fussing. I don't know if you have been in this type of relationship or not, but maybe you have been around it. Do you know those couples that seem to fuss all the time? They are never satisfied with anything the other person does. They talk to each other very aggressively. From an outsider's point of view, it seems emotionally abusive, but when one of them tries to leave, the other one acts like they are losing their best friend. Well that's actually true; they are losing their best friend. In this type of relationship, we as men have found an outlet valve. We have subconsciously set up a system that enables us to vent. Have you ever heard the expression, "taking it out on the closest people to you?" That's what's going on here. Sometimes we deal with pressure, issues, drama, struggles, and issues in our life that are constantly on our mind or just put us in a bad mood on a regular basis. As a man, when we come home, we need a release from all these things; we need to vent. Because we struggle to deal with emotions, some of us don't know how to sit down and say, "Baby, this is what's going on, this is how I feel."

What we really desire is for someone to rub our heads and say it's going to be okay, but we're taught as kids to suck it up, deal with it, and not cry. Even though men are symbols of strength, a lot of us aren't wired to be able to deal with all these different emotions internally. We're just not capable of brushing everything off. Unfortunately, what happens? We use our mate as an emotional punching bag. Our constant complaining and fussing is just the macho version of crying and venting. Seeing the person that we are close to sparks something inside us that makes us want to break down and lean on them emotionally. Because we are ruined emotionally, when we start to feel that fuzzy feeling, we battle against it. When the person receiving this abuse gets enough and tries to leave, we see the one positive thing in our lives walking away and we cannot let that happen under any circumstances. We set aside our emotional hang-ups to keep in place the one thing that offers us emotional stability. We are now willing to show our emotions because the consequence of losing you outweighs the uncomfortable feeling of showing emotions. This is definitely a seesaw type of relationship and can drive you crazy.

How do you handle this type of relationship? There are two options. The first option is for us to change it ourselves. To do this, don't accept our negative output but instead force us to discuss what's going on with us. Set aside communication time daily and don't respond to or reward any negative commentary. We honestly don't want to be that way, but catering to our attitude will never repair it. Basically, don't take any mess from us. It's not that we don't respect and care for you, we just don't reflect it consistently. Other than internally handling the problem, the only other option is talking to someone that can offer us professional guidance. A psychologist or counselor can offer advice, tips, and ideas on how to deal with what is being held in emotionally. They can also offer advice on communicating with each other. A professional could also be someone that is easier to talk to and vent off frustration with, as compared to your mate. If these things seem too far-fetched and too much trouble, then the final option would simply be to leave and stay gone. Remember, we are talking about break ups.

Break Up to Wake Up

We all are familiar with the idea of break up to make up, but a lot of people deal with a process I call break up to wake up. These guys tend to *sleep* on how good a person you are when you are together, but when you end it they *awaken* and become overly active in their attempts to get you back. The difference between the previous example and this one is the substitution of negativity with complacency. A lot of times we are actually happy with our relationship, but we might not show it. When we are in pursuit of you we go above and beyond, but once we've got you we go into chill mode. I know every woman that just read that is asking herself, *Why is that?* Well let me explain it this way: men are looking for that trophy wife/girlfriend. We are competing, fighting, kicking, and punching to get that dime piece that every other guy wishes they had. When we acknowledge you as being that valuable, you love the attention and you don't see anything other than our valiant efforts to impress and acquire you. In our minds, it's like football season, and you are our Super Bowl trophy. Our dating life with you is our football season, and every date is the game of the week. In pursuit of the trophy, we practice and train to become better, and we battle to win week in and week out. Its grueling, strenuous, hard work, but the prize is worth it. After months of pursuing this quest, you reward our efforts and crown us champion and hand over our trophy: yourselves. Just like football, once we've won the trophy, the season is over. There is no longer an incentive to continue with the rigorous process we're currently undergoing. We've reached our goal. That's a real deal fact for a lot of men; the goal is not a long term, happy, healthy relationship, the goal is simply to establish a relationship for the sake of simply saying, "Look what I did." Once we have that, we don't work inside the relationship because we only planned to work up to the relationship. It's all about the acquisition. It's all about conquering.

Think about this. How many of you who have played sports in school or have kids that play sports, and have trophies from those sports in your homes? Of all those trophies, how many of them are sitting on a shelf dusty? Exactly! The trophy is a symbol of a conquest, but it's a conquest completed. Once you as a trophy wife or trophy girlfriend have been acquired, you'll find yourself getting dusty. You are placed on our life's mantle as a display. We may refer to you every once in a while as a flashback to our glory days, but that only amounts to brief and random sparks of interest that will not suffice for the constant nurturing you desire.

The second half of this concept is triggered by the break up process. When you break up with your mate in this situation, you start a new season. Our reign as champs has ended, and it puts us in the mindset to defend our title and repeat as back-to-back champions. Although we sat back in our own arrogance thinking we didn't have to make any more efforts, when you announce our previous champion status is now in jeopardy, we jump back into training camp and are ready to fight to not turn our trophy over to one of our competitors. The male ego dreads the thought of his arch rival (any other man) hoisting the trophy he previously held. A man also realizes how much he actually likes being your winner and will be willing to do whatever it takes to keep his title. The disconnection that we have with women in this situation is that you as women like us to know your value up front and never lose sight of it. We actually do know your value, which is why we pursued you in the first place. As far as losing sight of it, we really haven't lost sight of you, we just have blurry vision. When you walk out that door, all of a sudden things get clearer.

As a woman, you have to right to leave any relationship, especially if you don't feel appreciated. You also have the right to allow or deny a second chance for us to make it right. What I would like to share with you in helping you make that decision is that a man whose tasted victory has experienced something that will forever change him for the better. If he makes the winning three-point shot, scores the winning touchdown, or hits a grand slam homerun to win the big game, he's definitely going to want the ball in his hands every time the game is on the line. His confidence in high pressure situations and his big game experience are advantages an unproven rookie doesn't possess. When you're looking at what you want in your relationship, a veteran might be worth keeping on your team.

Break Up to Break Up

Another issue you may have to deal with in the break up process is actually breaking up. Be cautious with dealing with the guy that wants to remain friends after the relationship is over. As adults, you should be able to remain civil, respectful, and friendly after a break up, but you need to really examine the "we're still friends" concept very closely before agreeing to this post-relationship arrangement. First off, there are a few questions and concerns you should have. What's his motivation? What's the benefit? What are the boundaries? Sometimes you build such a good friendship with a person that you attempt a romantic relationship and for whatever reasons it just doesn't work. However, the friendship was the base of the relationship from the get-go and it's merely transitioning back to being best buds from a place you probably shouldn't have ventured off to in the first place. In that scenario, that's totally fine. No hard feelings, no confusion.

The reason a friend seems like a likely candidate for a lover is because you get along so well, they're dependable, they're loyal, and they're trustworthy. Those characteristics aren't just readily available in all people. The other thing is that your friends love you unconditionally. As friends with the opposite sex, you don't easily find that in the people you date, so you attempt a quick fix and date your friend. Unfortunately, friends to lovers can be a difficult transition sometimes, and when it doesn't work, I think it's a good thing to hold on to the beautiful friendship you had initially. For every other scenario, keep in mind of what we are discussing: breaking up, separating, taking apart, severing, dismantling, discontinuing, etc. To put it in layman terms: it should be the end.

People come into your life for a reason, for a season, or for a lifetime, and it would serve you well to identify which early on. When a guy wants to remain friends, it could be for some sexual benefit. That way of thinking is going to go directly to what boundaries you have set. If you allow that benefit system to exist after the relationship, that's your choice, and hopefully you and he can handle that. It could also be he has hopes of being able to win you back. This is a noble gesture and sometimes works out, but sometimes space after a breakup does more for repairing and refocusing than lingering. Sometimes you just need to clear your head and see things from outside the relationship to see how it looks to you. When you're inside of a relationship, there are too many things blocking your view. His thought process is related to his motivation. Besides that, the question would be what's in it for you? What do you have to gain by remaining friends and what exactly is that person's definition of friends? When you look at everything from a different perspective, it's probably just best to move on and just be cordial whenever you do cross each other's paths.

Break Up to Ache Up

The last concept I want to discuss is what I called break up to ache up. We just talked about the benefits, or the lack thereof, of remaining in each other's lives, but what about those people who do so without agreeing to it? What about those people that say they are trying to remain in your life, but really they are just trying to remain in your business. I call this break up to ache up. I'm referring to the guy who keeps tabs on you after you're separated and is constantly getting his feelings hurt by what he exposes himself to. This is the guy that says he knows you are broken up, but he calls your phone constantly. Then, when you don't answer as often as he thinks you should, he feels he's being ignored. What about the guy who you are no longer with that constantly makes references to your history with him, and makes insinuations toward you guys getting back together. When you don't respond or deny his advances he feels rejected and proceeds to tell you how wrong you are. Seriously, dude? This guy will also be the guy that wants every other guy to think that you are still together, or that you are in some way or another his property. All he's doing is not letting go and causing himself unnecessary pain. Hence the term, break up to ache up.

The ending of a relationship that was ever worth anything, is painful. Whether it's a job, a relationship, or just a weekend getaway, anything that you enjoy brings you grief when it ends. Everyone dreads the grieving process associated with the passing of something we love. However, that's life, and only the fearful and the foolish attempt to avoid it. Some guys hang on after a breakup, because they don't want to accept that it's over. In their mind, they have the illusion and delusion that you are still together. They are attempting to avoid the pain that is sure to follow after the break up. What's so ironic is that in attempt to avoid pain, they create more pain than if they would have just faced the situation as is.

Have you ever broken up with the guy that tries to play off your sympathy by talking about how good things used to be and how he's so hurt now. When you tell him that's the past, he thinks your discrediting what you did have. Ache! This guy also always has a million questions about your current relationship status. When you tell him you're dating, getting to know someone, or simply interested in meeting new people, he's hurt to the max and wants to blow up on you. Ache! God forbid you actually start a new relationship. He becomes overly compulsive about your whereabouts and how serious you are with the new guy. He will always have his opinion of how the new guy isn't enough for you. I wonder who he would suggest is good enough. Ache! All that this guy is doing is constantly exposing himself to pain and heartache that he doesn't have to. This is very unhealthy and can be dangerous. They fear having to face the grief associated with separation. Because they are trying to avoid the grief of that person leaving their lives, they are (ironically) ensuring that outcome to be more and more inevitable. By trying so hard to not lose that person, they are pushing them further and further away. It's also a form of obsession. The person they are not letting go of has become an idol to them. They have made a god out of that person. The Bible says in Exodus 20:3, "You shall have no other gods before me." Why? Well, when you make something other than God your god, you are highly susceptible to the wiles of the devil. When you are obsessed with something, you must have it by any means. It controls you. It dominates you.

If you are dealing with this type of guy, it starts off as being annoying. A lot of times, you're sympathetic because you care that he is hurting. What you need to realize is that no matter how nice you try to be, unless you are going to give in to what he desires, you're just nurturing a growing problem. The longer you stay out of reality, the harder reality is to accept when you're forced to face it. If you really want to help him and yourself, distance yourself as much as possible and don't give in. If this gets out of hand, then take the steps you have to in order to protect yourself. This situation is the foundation to the stalking, harassing, and domestic abuse and homicides that have become so common these days. Some of these guys believe that you are their property. Their self-esteem is so low that you validate them, and they can't handle feeling inadequate. I know you might think this guy you went to high school with, or the nice guy from church, or the coach of your son's soccer team would never stalk you or harm you. The truth is that being functional in society doesn't exempt you from having dysfunctions.

How many times have you heard someone say, *I never thought he would do something like that?* You never know what a person is capable of. Still not convinced? Well what if I told you that I used to be this guy? What if I told you I had a problem letting go in relationships and I've stalked girls, and assaulted girls and their new boyfriends? What if I told you I had several restraining orders placed on me? What if I told you my insecurities led to anger management issues that caused me to act out violently in response to rejection? Would you believe that I was the guy kicking in doors, making harassing phone calls, and threatening people's lives? Well I was. Surprised? Never saw that coming did you? Well the reality of it is that this mindset is a spiritual flaw, and a mental illness. I had to both seek God and a psychiatrist to overcome those issues. My exes will testify to the horror of ending a relationship with me, but since I got help (spiritual and professional), the exes will tell you quite a different story. I expose this about myself to educate you and to maybe save someone's daughter or mother from being senselessly hurt or worse. The devil is busy in today's society and he's exploiting all of our shortcomings. If you are dealing with a person that shows these signs, don't take it lightly. Know your worth and always do what's best for you, your family, and subsequently the ex-lover you're dealing with. Like I said before, nothing in life is certain or promised to you. Some losses you can recover from, some are permanent. Let go and let God.

Chapter Nine

SEX

the Non-Factor

Sex is such a small word to have such major implications. It's simply amazing to think of how broad a spectrum it covers: from our favorite form of personal entertainment, to the most taboo word amongst our friends and associates, to the process in which life itself is conceived. When I say sex carries major importance, if not the most importance in a relationship, no one should be surprised. However, what if told you that sex carries very little importance in relationships to a man, would that catch your attention? To further confuse you, what if I told you sex is very important and not important at all, both at the same time? Are you curious yet? Let's talk about sex.

The Truth About Sex

The truth about sex from a man's perspective is twofold. In most cases it's a necessity in our relationships, but at the same time, it's the last detail of the relationship we think about when we are ready to move on. Basically, we won't stay without it, but we won't stay because of it. Now you see? Women aren't the only complicated ones. In a relationship, we desire you to view sex as our own personal, intimate, special, sacred bond that only we share, but if we're caught having sex outside the relationship, we refer to it as meaningless and something that just happened. We would have you believe that no one has ever "sexed" us so good before you, but are quick to try to convince you to do some of the things that the ones before you have done. We as men always want to claim a woman sexually, demanding that her goods belong solely to us, but still complain when it comes to the upkeep of the woman those goods are attached to. Why are we so contradicting when it comes to sex? Well it's because over time, the concept of sex has contradicted itself. It's not just men's fault either, ladies. Sex has become both important and unimportant in relationships, and I'm going to tell you why and how we men view it.

Why It's Important

First off, sex is important, period. Take away any particular gender's viewpoint, and look at this at face value. Sex is the most intimate encounter that the members of a relationship can have. In its purest form, which is intimacy, sex can literally transfer the emotions of one partner unto the other. It creates a bond between you and your mate that is personal, specific, unique, pleasurable, fun, and it offers an emotional, physical, and mental pallet for you to build on endlessly. So before we even dissect reasons as to why men find it important, we have to respect the power it carries all on its own.

I've told you a million times in this book already, and hopefully it's starting to sink in: men are fairly simple and barbaric so the main reason sex is important to us is fairly simple and barbaric. On the simple side, sex is physically pleasurable. It's the best feeling we ever encounter in our entire lives. I want you to imagine eating your favorite food, at your favorite restaurant, followed behind with your favorite dessert, while listening to your favorite song, and conversing with your favorite friend, about your most favorite topic. Multiply that feeling by a hundred then multiply that feeling by a thousand. See how that feels? Well you're still not even close to how sex feels to us. From the second we stop seeing little girls as yucky playmates, to looking at them as objects of curiosity, we are on a road to realizing there are some things my football buddies just can't do for me. As a woman, it's one of those things that set you apart from the other things in our life. The intimate encounter of sex is personalized to us and only us, and stands alone and unique, unlike any other thing that I partake in. It sets a stage for you to demand your one on one attention. It forces us to put down all other distractions or things that would demand our time and attention, and focus solely on you. It leads to conversation, connection, and chemistry between the members of a relationship, and helps to de-stress relationships from the pressures life can often place on them.

The second reason it's important to us is because it boosts our ego. This is on the barbaric side of the house. It validates us as a man and makes us feel like the king of our jungle. I'm surprised we don't literally grunt and beat on our chest after sex because that's the kind of alpha male reinforcement it gives us. That's why we become protective a lot of times, because we are instinctively territorial. Honestly, not so much because we love our woman, as much as because we want you to respect our territory. As a woman, you can take advantage of this truth, because it can be used to encourage and motivate us. When I come home from a long day at work and you got a bath drawn for me, some smothered pork chops on the stove, and you're wearing that skimpy-green-you-gonna-get-lucky tonight dress I like, I feel like I can work 1,000 more days to make sure you're happy.

You ladies need to get this, so listen up. As a man I need my woman to do three things: feed me, freak me, and free me. I don't care how intelligent, elite, or upscale you think your man is, if you don't cater to those three things, you are going to have a problem. And I don't care how little potential you think your man has, if you do those three things, he can be somebody. If my woman keeps a good meal on my table, makes good love to me on a regular basis, and doesn't try to restrict me from my own personal time, she will never have to worry about anything; ever. I will make sure she is happy, stable, secure, loved, protected, and provided for. This is so crucial. I really need you to understand this, so excuse me for a second while I get a little raw, because you can't afford to miss this. If a woman can lay me back in a recliner in front of a 56' TV with the New Orleans Saints versus the Atlanta Falcons game on, place a double-decker grilled ham and cheese sandwich that she prepared herself in my left hand and the remote control in my right hand, and tell me how sexy I am while laying her head on my chest without her ponytail blocking the screen I would probably buy her an engagement ring during halftime. I wouldn't even notice another woman because you have met all my needs in a way that I'm tuned out to anything outside of you. I don't care if you're dating Colin Powell or Pookie from Ninth Street, the same principle applies without prejudice. If you don't grasp that, your relationship is subject to "interference" at any moment. You can be intoxicated on love all you want, but please take a shot of reality as a chaser.

Why It's Not Important

Now after telling you how important sex is, I know you're wondering why I would come back and say it's not important. Well what I said before still reigns true in reference to its importance, but the reason it's not important is because it can't stand alone. Contrary to popular belief, our brains are not guided by our genitals. We do enjoy sex and it does give us an ego boost, but if all you have to offer is sex, then you are guaranteed to not be in a healthy relationship. Men are like grown little boys, and we do get bored with things fast. We love our X-box, but we do have multiple games. Sex is one of the things we love about our relationship with you, but it can't be the only thing. You need to be able to stimulate us mentally as well. You need to be the kind of woman we are proud of. You need to offer us stability in our homes. You need to be the kind of woman to demand respect. You need to be the kind of role model I want my daughter to be around. All these things add up to the reason why I look forward to continually having sex with you. The absence of these things leave you with only a sexual connection and you'll end up on the shelf like the 2010 version of our favorite video game. If your sex does keep me, then I have issues and you have short-changed yourself dramatically. Any man that is controlled by sex is either addicted to sex, or has a self-esteem issue where he feels not many women want him. In this case, the sex addict will most likely screw anything with a pulse and a phone number, and drama is bound to follow. The low self-esteem guy is not equipped to help you reach your full potential as person because your time is consumed by constantly trying to build him up.

You see, ladies, sex in a relationship is contradictory. It should be something you offer freely, but it should be something we have to work for. Your goods should belong to only us, but it should be controlled by only you. It should be pricelessly valued like something we are not worthy of, but be presented to us like we are the only ones that are worthy. When you get that combination down, you have begun the process of making sex a healthy part of your relationship.

The Real Truth About Sex

Now, there is one other factor that I have to discuss in reference to sex. This is going to blow your mind too. If you are *not* married, your decision to have sex is a recreational one. Let me repeat this: If you are not married, sex is only recreational! A Biblical fact is that sex outside of marriage is fornication, which is a sin. You are not receiving all your blessings from God when you are living in sin. Yes, we all sin and no sin is greater than the other, but this is still sin nevertheless. I say this so that you can understand that maybe the reason you are having difficulty in your relationship is because you are doing things out of order. Do we all have premarital sex? I can't say all of us are, but I would be willing to guess at least ninety-five percent of us are, and that number might be a little low. However great the number, it doesn't change the spiritual principle applied to it. God's grace and mercy abound, and we are forgiven for our sins when we repent, but to constantly indulge in the same sin does carry some sort of penalty. I say this to speak a truth we tend to like to sweep under the rug. We all enjoy sex, and conveniently ignore the fact that it was not designed as a pre-marital source of entertainment.

A lot of times in relationships, two people are meant for each other, but it seems like you face all kinds of hang-ups and hindrances that keep you from getting over the hump. A lot of times, it's the devil operating in your relationship freely because you are out of position and not under your covering. At some point, you have to mutually decide you want more, and be willing to purify and sanctify your relationship. I personally think it speaks volumes that a person is willing to deny their own flesh in not only a pursuit of personal preservation, but also with an interest on ensuring a long-lasting, healthy, and blessed relationship with me, but maybe I'm just old fashioned. Now, is this easy to do? Heck no! However, it's not impossible, and could be the course of action that takes you from point A to point B. Either way, treat each other with honor and respect, and not merely as objects of sexual pleasure, and life just kind of works itself out from there.

Chapter Ten

WHY MEN CHEAT

(Don't Read This Chapter First…Be Patient)

Why Do Men Cheat? This is a question that's always asked whenever you discuss relationships. I've heard so many different and creative answers to this question that you wouldn't believe half of it if I told you. With that being said, let me put my two cents in it. I think there are several things associated with cheating, but I believe all roads lead back to a basic foundation. In my opinion, cheating stems from three causes:

1. Physical stimulation – natural, animalistic, man to woman attraction. (i.e. turned on, horny, aroused by touch or sight)

2. Mental stimulation – stroking of the ego or boosting of the self-esteem (i.e. flattery, flirtation, compliments, insinuation, or submission)

3. Spiritual/Mental flaw – demonic strongholds, generational curses, or mental/moral defect (i.e. nymphomania, spirit of lust, whoredom)

Basically, the act of cheating is generated from a seed planted in one of these three areas. Now to keep this simple, we're not going to get into number three. This book is all about thought processes, and I can't successfully examine the third source because it's not based on cognitive thought. Those things are tied to demonic soul ties and mental illness. If you are dating a whore, there is something wrong internally that needs to be repaired. They aren't really operating under their own free will. They are consumed and possessed by something greater than themselves, and what I'm discussing here doesn't apply to them. They need intervention and intercession. I can only offer this to those that fall in that category: seek whatever spiritual and professional help you can in order to break free of that bondage. Now as far as the rest of us, it's fairly simple.

Rule #1 – This is simple human nature. A man desires a woman, key word being desire. It's an actual need, no different than water and shelter. Be very careful of the ones who say "I don't need sex." What they are probably saying is "I don't need sex with you." I know it feels good to think that someone is waiting on you, and some of us can wait a long time, but that need will eventually win. Sometimes, people can go a long time without it because they have no choice. They just aren't able to acquire it from any place they feel comfortable, but not being able to do it and not doing it is two different things. And those people do have sex with themselves, but that's another book. Now, women can endure a lot longer than men because of the emotional aspect that you require in order to engage sexually, and as a matter of fact, that should help you understand our dilemma. Ladies, think about your loneliest night. You have had a few glasses of wine, read one of your steamy novels, and watched *Love and Basketball* for the thousandth time. You're tuned into Luther Vandross radio on Pandora, and there's a light rain hitting your roof and window pane. You got the pumpkin spice scented candles lit and you look at the clock on the nightstand and it says two a.m. something inside you is happening and you just can't relax. You try to fall asleep, but you just toss and turn. So you sit up in bed, pick up your cell phone, and scroll through your contacts. You say you're just playing with your phone, but we all know better. Then as you scroll down through your phone, you come across a name that catches your attention: Joseph. Joseph is the doctor you've been dating sparingly for the past two months. He's always been real nice, respectful, and the perfect gentleman. You think to yourself, he does get off work late; maybe you should give him a call, *just to talk*. Now, hold up right there. You see how you ladies are feeling right now? Well, men walk around at that point 24/7. When you pick up the phone and call Joseph, the second he sees your name appear on his phone at two a.m., he's already on the same page as you. The mere thought of what could happen, places him at a position of ready. We don't need all the candles, mood setters, and slow music. All we really need is permission. I know some of you don't want to see your man in that light, because he's so romantic with you, but it's the truth. We are barbaric and animalistic. When your man is romantic with you, cherish him. He's that way because he finds you worth it, but don't put your guards down. As romantic as he may be, I bet you if you pulled him into a restaurant bathroom and told him you want him now, you would see a side of your man you didn't think existed. I say all that to say, that we are not nasty and trifling, we are just designed differently when it comes to our physical nature. We get aroused easier than you do, and although we do have a decent amount of self-restraint, we can get pushed passed a point of no return. And that's the key; knowing where that point of no return is. It's different for each man, but it does exist in every man.

Rule #2 – Now, if women like to feel loved and desired, then men like to feel like they're "The Man." Nothing does more for a man that boosting his ego. If you notice, the best athletes in the world have the worst attitudes in their sport. Michael Jordan, Kobe Bryant, Tiger Woods, they all come off as buttholes to other competitors because they have enormous egos that give them that killer instinct. They're feeling themselves. As a man, when you are getting your ego stroked, it feels like someone is injecting you with cocaine and ice cream at the same time. You feel empowered. You feel overly sufficient. You feel above average. You feel more than adequate. It's downright intoxicating. It's the same way being loved makes you ladies feel. When a woman tells us we're fine and sexy, even if we're 250 pounds overweight, she instantly has our attention. When she says she's impressed with how smart we are, even if we rode the short bus to school, we still buy into it. And if she ever insinuates that she's turned on by us, we become bumbling idiots, following her around wherever she goes. Some of us might try to play it cool, but internally we are happy as cats with milk. That's why we turn around and brag to our homeboys about how you are impressed by us, because we are so happy, we just had to tell somebody.

When a woman flirts with us, the more we entertain it, the more control she has in the situation. The adrenaline we release from our egotistical massage becomes more addictive than any drug, and in our minds we need another hit. As a woman, when you're in a relationship with us, understand that we do have a "drug habit" due to our addiction to ego-boosting, and even though you're our main supplier; we often will seek out other dealers out of convenience. You see, what's happening here, is it's not about you as our woman. It's solely about us. You have done nothing wrong at all. We are totally engaged in a situation that's completely unrelated to you. If we don't stop this process, we trick ourselves into thinking we deserve this attention because we're so great. It doesn't mean we love you any less, it's just that at that moment, we choose to love ourselves more. Let me give you an exercise to further go into depth with this subject and see if we can understand it better.

The Question

I have a question for the ladies. I need you to loosen up your minds, give me a little creative liberty, and answer this question to yourself honestly. Here it is:

If your man was 1,000 miles away on a business trip, and Halle Berry, Tyra Banks, or Jennifer Lopez walked into his hotel room, wearing only lingerie, and demanded sex from him, would he do it?

How you answer that question will tell you a lot about your man, but it will also tell you a lot about yourself. For some added fun, ask your man directly if he would do it (now I'm just being messy).

Some women will answer that question and say, "Any man would do it because they wouldn't get caught." If you think your man cheating is predicated on him getting away with it, then you either have enough knowledge and history of him to know he's a cheater, your views are biased because all you've been with is cheaters in the past, or you yourself are a cheater. Anytime you use words like *any* or *all*, it's a generalization. There are very few things that apply to all of any group of people, so to use those type phrases mean it's true for all the people you have experienced. Not knowing another option is not proof of its non-existence. When a woman has that mentality, as a man it makes us feel devalued. Our efforts at being faithful seem unappreciated because we're subject to the penalties of a crime someone else committed. I understand your baby daddy was a dog, and the guys before and after him were the same way, but I'm not them. I knew a guy in the military named Robert Kelly that oddly enough was from Chicago, and he couldn't sing a note. Point being, just because men are alike in some ways (male, mid 20s, and dating you), don't mean they're identical. If by chance you are getting the same type of guys and having the same type of experiences, maybe you should change something about yourself. I personally hate being accused of something I know I didn't do, and I despise even more being accused of something I know I wouldn't do. I guess maybe *any* man would do it, but I'm not just *any* man, and you would be surprised how many men are more like me and less like Spike, King, Spot, and Rover.

Some women will respond to the question by saying, "He'll do it just because it's Halle Berry, and it's a once in a lifetime opportunity." This reply goes directly to how valuable your man makes you feel, and how valuable you yourself feel you are. Do you somehow think that Halle Berry is a better woman than you? Do you think her qualities and traits are more valuable than what you bring to the table? Yes, she is strikingly beautiful, but don't you think your man looks at you with the same awe? Beauty is in the eye of the beholder and it is not limited to outward physical appearance. What else does he know about J-Lo, other than that she has a pretty face, and possesses remarkable curves. Is she a better mother than you? Does she have great conversation? Can she cook lasagna as good as you do? There are so many other things involved in a relationship that light our fire and keeps the sparks between us. Is Tyra Banks free from bad relationships herself? Has she ever been cheated on or unappreciated? Does she struggle to find a mate that is equally yoked? How many failed relationships has she been in? Is she currently reading this book right along with you? (If she is, Hi Tyra, how are you? Call me when you get a chance.) Not only is this a question of your value, it's a question of your man's value. As a guy, I like to think that I'm on the same level as any woman. I am not such a lesser being that to play kissy-face with a celebrity would be the highlight of my life. That makes me sound like when Marcia Brady met Davey Jones. I would like to think that I would need more than status in my mate in order to want to venture into something that could jeopardize my current situation. What you don't know is, that yes your man might cheat with Halle Berry, and you have put her on such a high pedestal that you can accept that, but the reality of it is, he'll do the same thing with Tasha from around the corner. If he thinks Halle is outside of his league, the thought of being with her will appeal to Rule #2. His ego will be boosted by having shared this escapade with a woman he never thought he could ever have had. However, remember cheating is not about the woman he cheats with, it's about him. It's a selfish decision that he makes for himself. If he thinks he deserves that attention, he's going to get it from whomever. The decision to not cheat is about him deciding he wants to honor his commitment. He needs to see that what he's built is more valuable than the woman threatening to destroy it. In my opinion, yes, the opportunity for me and Halle Berry to sleep together is a once in a lifetime opportunity…for Halle.

Another response to that question might be, "A man is a man, and a naked woman in his room can seduce him into doing it." That is a true statement. Remember Rule #1: we are men, and the most basic parts of our DNA attract us to women. The way you walk, the way you talk, the way you smell, even the way you stand still does something to us. God intended for us to be attracted to you. It's part of the reproductive process and the cycle of life. The catch is that those desires come from the flesh and the control of those desires comes from the spirit. It creates balance. The question now is how do you control those desires? Theoretically you can and you can't. Some men are stronger than others and can withstand more physical temptation, but I don't care who you are, eventually every man will succumb to sexual stimulation, period. I know women will take that statement and run with it, and say, "So it's true all men cheat." No. I didn't say that. All men have the *potential* to cheat. Potential does not constitute intent. You see, women think that men plan to cheat. You think we plot and plan to figure out how we can get us a side piece or something new, and still maintain our home. You would somehow believe we got a hotel in the same hotel as Halle Berry on purpose, and we purposely bumped into Tyra in the lobby, or went out of our way to get noticed by J-Lo. That's false. Contrary to popular belief, most men don't plan to cheat; we just fail to plan to not cheat.

If I know I'm in a relationship, and my single friends and I are going to Vegas, I need to take the proper steps beforehand to avoid a negative situation from arising. I need to get my own hotel room. I need to call you often and accept your calls. I need to go to the casino floor and play slots when the rest of the fellas go to the strip club. I need to give you my hotel name and room number, and I need to not buy into to the concept that what happens in Vegas stays in

Vegas. Herpes or HIV won't stay in Vegas, no matter what the commercial says. Basically, I need to put myself in position to where it would be very difficult to do anything naughty. Not because I'm weak, but because what I have is worth the precautionary measures. If I know the girl at work likes me, I don't need to read the non-work related emails and texts she sends me. Yes, it feels good to have a young intern show me attention (Rule #2), that's why I have to make sure she doesn't work with me alone. I have to tell her from the first incident to keep it professional. I could even go as far as to tell my significant other about her advances and flirtations. What that does is give me an out. Once I know that my woman is aware of it, I better not be caught within one hundred feet of this woman, or else. I know it's funny, but those steps keep you from getting caught up. Because what happens is this: she has already appealed to my ego by flirting with me every day and Rule #2 has been satisfied. Then we she dances with me to Juvenile's "Back That Thang Up" at the office Christmas party you couldn't attend, Rule #1 comes into play and now you have a problem. It doesn't matter if it's Fred and Barney, or Bishop Whomever and Pastor So and So, if you don't remove yourself from temptation you will succumb to it.

Now don't fret, because it's not that simple to get caught up. There is a grading curve by which this is judged. As a woman, you can't control what we do. Like I've been stressing, cheating is a selfish act. It's not about you. All you can do is increase or decrease the odds of it happening. Each man is equipped with a temptation hour glass. This hour glass symbolizes the amount of time we are able to resist temptation without giving in. As a woman, how good you are and how much we love you will add sand to our hour glass. At the same time, how poorly you treat us, how little you stroke our egos, or the more we feel unappreciated, the amount of sand decreases. When Halle walks into my hotel room, I may have thirty minutes to be exposed to that situation and resist it. If I get up immediately, walk out, and go downstairs and call you from the lobby, I have managed to not make a mistake I would later regret. Some guys could actually be in that environment, and actually have an hour long conversation with Tyra as to why he doesn't want to, and walk out of there just in the nick of time. Then again, some guys couldn't even look through the peephole and see J-Lo standing there without getting naked. I mean you just have to know your man. At the end of the day, keep pouring sand into a good man and he'll do the right thing. Now fellas, I got a little something to share with you. It's time to wake up.

Wake Up Call for the Fellas

A man with a woman is more attractive than a man without. Not because women want what other women have, or because women always want what they can't have. Actually, once a man is paired with a woman, a real woman, she grooms us to be better. He walks differently, talks differently, and has a different confidence. He has a different swagger. His style of dress is more appealing, his haircut and mustache better fit him, his conversation is stronger, and his mannerisms are even sexy. Basically, what you are seeing is a man that has been tailored by his woman to what a man should be. He's been refined and polished over a length of time by his woman, unknowingly, and made into a better man. To an outside woman, that's the difference between a base model vehicle, and a vehicle with all the newest features and amenities on it, without having to pay the cost of the upgrade. The issue for a man is that in his vain ego, he thinks he's getting all this newfound attention because he's all that, and he actually will take this prideful attitude home and start placing new demands on his current woman. He now feels she needs to step her game up because she is now somehow lucky to have him. In reality, his ignorance eludes him; he is actually lucky to have her. Her efforts, commitment, dedication, and investment into this man is paying benefits that he thinks he's entitled to, and not the one who actually made the investment. That's like the cashier at the convenience store thinking he's entitled to half the profit on the winning lottery ticket you bought from him. Many times you see a man who has left his former wife or woman, and the new woman is an obvious downgrade, and you wonder why he left his good thing for her. Well, in actuality he didn't. Like I said before, that man was taken from a base model vehicle to a vehicle with all kinds of after-market upgrades. He has shiny rims now, tinted windows, a new sound system, DVD players and screens – the works. When he puts himself up for sale because he thinks he has some interested buyers, they are attracted to the car as is. Unbeknownst to him, the owner, which is the woman, releases the car for sale but removes all the bells and whistles they have added. Now the potential buyers are no longer interested, but he's already committed to selling. So he's then forced to go with whoever's willing to purchase him. In the end, he has to face the fact that without the care, investment, and maintenance of the original owner you're simply a used car.

I say this to say to the fellas: it's very hard to maintain a successful relationship. I know this book is probably going to be read by a majority of women, but remember, we are single too. Sometimes you need to hear some things about yourself before you can realize them. If you are in a relationship or about to start one, make sure that's what you really want. Once you've decided that's what you want, treat it like a prized possession. When you think about your woman, give her the same love, honor, and respect you would give your daughter or mother, because God says if you were to marry her, she would become more important than both of those people. A lot of us have gotten away from our roles and we are not successful in life because we don't have a firm foundation. Family is the foundation of life, and if we can't keep a girlfriend longer than six weeks the family we are supposed to build will never exist. At the end of the day, if I take money from you, I can replace it. If I take material possessions from you, I can replace them. But if I take your time and waste it, I can never give that back to you, and how precious every second is on this Earth. We are not perfect guys, never said we were, but we are held accountable and responsible. Let's do something different, and learn to be better men, especially to our women.

Prologue

YOUR BEST RELATIONSHIP

S o now we've come to the end of this journey through relationships and as I look back through this book I must say I have really enjoyed it. As I sit here, I think to myself, if I had to leave you guys with one thing to remember, what would it be? And it's this: You have all read this book from start to finish, and throughout the course of this book you have agreed and disagreed with some things. You have laughed at some things you found to be true, and maybe you have cried for the same reason. Hopefully some of you were inspired. Hopefully some of you were educated. Hopefully some of you were simply entertained. I know a lot of you have picked up this book because you were looking for a few things to help you in this crazy business of trying to build relationships. And over the course of these chapters, you may have come to like me. You may have found my words to be clever, and my point of view to be in line with what you believe. You may have gotten halfway through this book and told your home girl she needs to get it and catch up to you so you can discuss it. You may have taken something I wrote and instantly applied it to your life and your situation.

You may have broken up with someone that wasn't good for you, or came to appreciate someone that was. Some of you may have emailed me to tell me thanks for writing this book. Some of you may think I'm just crazy. However, there's a secret about this book I would like to share with you: It's nothing more than words from a dude with the same problems and issues that you have. I'm still figuring this relationship thing out daily, and I am nowhere near having all the answers, but I can refer you to someone who can really help you.

There's another book that was written a long time before mine. It's an oldie, but a goodie. It was written by a magnificent author, whose credentials far exceed mine. Of course the book I'm referring to is The Holy Bible, the author being God. You see, as intelligent as you may think I am this guy here looks at my thoughts as mere gibberish. Actually, everything in my book is plagiarized off of something he already wrote millennia ago. So much so, that I'm going to give him full credit for my work, and I'm going to pay him ten percent commission on all sales. What I'm trying to get you to understand is that we turn to the world for answers to our dilemmas. We deal with so much, that we are looking for a friend, a counselor, a book, a DVD, or anything that can help us along the way. What we have to realize is that there's a friend that has all the answers. There's a book that has all the instructions. There's a guy that you need to have a relationship with, before you can have a relationship with any other person. He should be your first love, because you were his. He will never cheat on you or let you down. He can love you like no other. He will teach you so much about yourself, and give you everything you desire and more. So as much as I appreciate you sharing in my experiences, I encourage you to properly invest in your own. Make God the head of your life, and watch how easy this relationship thing becomes. What better relationship can you be in, than a relationship with God? It's the best relationship I've ever had.

I humbly and sincerely thank you for supporting my work.

I love you all. Good luck and God Bless.

About the Author

Donald Thomas Jr. is a native of Lake Charles, Louisiana. He is a single dad of three kids and a veteran of the United States Army Reserve. Although he has held many different jobs throughout the years, he's most known as a promoter, serving as the Co-CEO of Southern Touch Entertainment. In his career as a promoter, he's grown from promoting local artists and events to promoting national acts in multiple markets and organizing national tours.

Donald comes from humble beginnings, growing up in the Carver Courts housing projects in the Goosport neighborhood of north Lake Charles. Even though financially challenged, he never saw limits on what he could accomplished. He credits his drive and determination to the hardworking attitude he witnessed displayed by his parents. In addition to hard work, the strong Christian environment and spiritual foundation established by his parents are credited for all of his successes in life. He believes "It doesn't matter where you start, God has the final say-so of where you finish."

As an author, his passion for writing is one that began in childhood. From writing short stories, to essays, to research papers in school, he discovered his enjoyment and talent of writing. Through his career he has written speeches, business proposals, scripts for television and radio ads, songs for musical artists, and currently writes a monthly magazine column called "I'm Just Saying." He has a passion for taking ideas and issues, and transferring them to the minds of the masses through literary works. Community and political issues, his religious beliefs, and the ins and outs of relationships are definitely some of his favorite topics when writing, but he has a broad base of subject matter when it comes to putting words together.

Donald was inspired to write this book because he believes family is the foundation of life. The strength found in the family unit sets a base in which generations upon generations can sprout happy and productive people from. However, if we never attain a healthy relationship with each other, we can never achieve that family unit. This book is his attempt to get passed the initial stage of getting to know each other, and learning how to love each other. He hopes that after reading this work, you will be more understanding of the thought process of the average guy, and better equipped to assist your potential mate in building a future.

FOLLOW THE LOVE ONLINE

 facebook.com/aregulardude

 twitter.com/a_regular_dude

FOR BOOKING/PRESS

iamtheregulardude@gmail.com